C000090187

Systematic Sociology: An Introduction To The Study Of Society

Karl Mannheim

Systematic Sociology

AN INTRODUCTION TO THE STUDY OF SOCIETY

Edited by

J. S. ERÖS
Lecturer in Political Institutions
University College of North Staffordshire

and

W. A. C. STEWART
Professor of Education
University College of North Staffordshire

PHILOSOPHICAL LIBRARY

New York

© *1957 by John Erös and W. A. C. Stewart*

Published in U.S.A. 1958
by Philosophical Library, Inc.,
15 East 40th Street, New York 16, N.Y.

All rights reserved

Made and printed in Great Britain by
William Clowes and Sons, Limited
London and Beccles

Contents

CONTENTS

PART 2
THE MOST ELEMENTARY
SOCIAL PROCESSES

CONTENTS

PART 3

SOCIAL INTEGRATION

PART 4

SOCIAL STABILITY AND SOCIAL CHANGE

CONTENTS

EDITORIAL ACKNOWLEDGEMENTS

We should like to express our gratitude to the University College of North Staffordshire for research grants awarded to us in connection with this work: to the Librarians of the College for their practical help and advice: and to Miss Mary Barraclough for her assistance in preparing the typescript of these pages.

Editorial Preface

When Karl Mannheim was proscribed by Hitler in 1933, like others on that first list he was at once offered academic posts in universities in different parts of the world. He came to London, and the book which follows is based on two of the courses of lectures that he gave in London: the first was given at the London School of Economics under the title *Systematic Sociology*, and the second elsewhere under the title *Social Structure*.

The first three parts of this book are based on the manuscript of Mannheim's lectures on systematic sociology, first delivered during the academic session 1934-35 and, in slightly modified form, during the following sessions. Part Four of this book is based on some of the lectures in a course on social structure delivered during the war years.

In editing the lectures on systematic sociology, we have considerably re-ordered the argument and re-phrased the text. A number of issues were raised as parentheses by Mannheim in giving the lectures, the relationship of which to the written text would not be easy to understand. We have in places omitted these comments so that the argument of the whole could be more clearly seen. Whatever the alterations and excisions we may have made, we have attempted to maintain the structural outline, the architecture of the argument.

In Part Four we have used Karl Mannheim's typescript without much alteration. However, we have not maintained the structural outline of the course of lectures on which this part of the book is based. The lectures covered a great variety of topics: the first lectures contained a shortened version of the topics dealt with in more detail in Part One of this book; several lectures dealt with what Mannheim himself called 'concrete issues' of modern society and thus do not fit into the frame-work of his systematic sociology, and finally there are a few lectures on 'problems of social stability and social change'—subjects which, according to the original syllabus of his lectures on systematic sociology, he wished to incorporate into his course on systematic sociology. It seems that considerations of time prevented Mannheim from analysing such problems as social control, social change, and social structure in his lectures at the London School of Economics, so that he decided to cover these problems within the framework of the other lecture course. We thought it fitting to restore Mannheim's original plan for a systematic sociology in this book and in doing this we have fulfilled a wish of Dr. Julia Mannheim.

We are grateful that Dr. Julia Mannheim allowed us the opportunity to undertake this work, and we are saddened by the thought that she did not live long enough to see it completed.

Karl Mannheim's Concept of a Systematic Sociology

In his introductory lecture to the systematic sociology lecture course (re-printed in this book as the Introduction) Karl Mannheim claims that the various forms of the 'living together of men' constitute the subject matter of analytical systematic sociology. This is, of course, only a preliminary definition, and a detailed study of this book shows that although an analysis of the different forms of human integration constitutes the central part of this systematic sociology, he also investigates psychological and cultural problems which may not at first sight seem directly connected with the problem of integration

xii

and with an analysis of the forms of the 'living together of men'.

Part One of this book deals with the problem of man and his psychic equipment. Here Karl Mannheim shows the unique plasticity of man's character and behaviour and analyses the processes which govern the distribution of his psychic energy. At the end of Part One a description of the main types of social attitudes and wishes forms a bridge between the psychological and sociological sections of the book, because a wish or an attitude is a more or less established response to an environment.

In Part Two, entitled 'The Most Elementary Social Processes', Mannheim analyses the social forms and processes which either bring people together or isolate them from one another or even induce them to act against one another. He deals here on the one hand with the processes which lead to the various forces of social integration and on the other hand with the phenomena of differentiation and individualisation. Mannheim's interest in the human personality, as it appears to be on the one hand group-centred and on the other individualised can be clearly seen throughout these chapters.

In Part Three of the book, 'The Sociology of Integration', however, he concentrates on the problems of human integration and attempts to give a systematic account of the different 'forms of human living together'. His description of human psychological development as it appears in Part One and his analysis of the integrating social processes in Part Two form an indispensable introduction to this third part of the book.

Finally in Part Four (which is based on the typescript of the lectures on social structure) the author analyses the social forces and institutions which create social stability, and discusses the theories relating to the factors of social change. His criticism of the Marxist theory of social change constitutes the central part of the concluding chapter.

We shall attempt here to give a brief analysis of the four main divisions into which this book, and Mannheim's systematic sociology, is divided, and shall begin with a discussion of the problems of man and his psychic equipment. Karl Mannheim attempted in these lectures a more systematic analysis of the psychological aspects of man and society than he had ever before essayed. Reading it at this distance of time, over twenty years after it was planned, it is not difficult to regard it as at least partly outmoded. The fashions have changed in psychology and in social philosophy. Where Mannheim describes personal development in the terms of transference of libido, the more recent work in America by Horney, Erikson, Sullivan or Alexander, or in this country the work of the Tavistock Clinic, has taken more account of social factors. Where Mannheim attempts to classify types of social integration or individualisation the tendency now in sociology is to undertake field work which relies for its methodology and verification on the case study method of social anthropology, the interview technique or on statistical analysis. Yet this section of the book should not be regarded as of historical interest only, but as a necessary chapter in the changing pattern of Mannheim's thought. It represents a synthesis of ideas and a method of analysis which can be indefinitely elaborated.

In considering man's psychic equipment Mannheim deals right at the start with the genetic bases of psychic energy and with the relationship between what may be termed instinct and what may be termed habit, with all the problems of learning attendant thereto. The emphasis on structure and relationism throughout Mannheim's writing ensures that he looks at the problems of perceiving, conceiving, experiencing, learning, knowing, as one interested in the dynamics of the processes, leaning to *gestalt* rather than connectionist or associationist interpretations. He says that associationism affords a descriptive model at a certain level of the processes of thought and behaviour, and such explicitness is to be welcomed for it represents a degree of conscious awareness of the process. However, such an account does not take into its reckoning the powerful basic experiences of life which become standards and give the personality a cohesion and unity which enable it to have 'initiative' in relation to learning and what the pragmatists call adjustment.

Mannheim's argument and methodology bring Freud and McDougall into the discussion; they also call in W. I. Thomas, who tried to meet the problem of the relationship between genetic endowment and social setting by postulating a number of wishes; they lean heavily upon MacIver. Any thoughtful reader can see that this links with pragmatic notions in philosophy and psychology on the one side and that on the other the fundamental questions here have been approached in a different way by neo-behaviourists like Hull and Skinner and eclectics like Tolman.

Mannheim's introductory comments on psychology in this book may be rudimentary in their psychoanalytic generalisations, but on closer examination the germs of the social expression of Freudian and gestaltist notions as they have since been developed are seen to be there. As Dr. Kecskemeti in his Introduction to an earlier volume in this series wrote:

'Sociology, then, had to emerge from isolation and achieve integration with other social sciences. In particular, "sociological psychology" had to be developed. This "sociological psychology", Mannheim held, had to utilise the results, insights and methods of various psychological schools, not only psychoanalysis. Above all, it had to maintain a social perspective; it had to differentiate itself from all individual psychology as such. "We cannot jump straight from the general

observation of individuals and their psychic mechanisms to the analysis of society. The psychology of
society is not a million times that of an individual." [1]

While Mannheim regards an examination of man's
psychic equipment as a necessary introduction to what
he calls sociology proper, he considers the sociology of
integration to be the central theme of the study.

At the beginning in his sociology of integration Mannheim draws our attention to the fundamental differences
between stable social groups and transient human agglomerations. He stresses that genuine social groups are
characterised by the existence of stable contacts between
their members. Examples of such groupings, based on
real personal relationships, are the family, the play
group, the educational group, the religious community,
the political party, and so on. The most striking example
of a transient agglomeration is the crowd. The unstable
character of crowds makes it impossible for real relationships to develop between the members. In stable social
groups, however, the behaviour of the members is shaped
by definite group traditions, inhibitions and ethical
standards. In transient agglomerations, like the crowd or
the public, the social traditions and ethical standards
which emerged within the stable groups, may tend to
disappear. The fact that members of stable social groups
can also meet within such unstable agglomerations as a
crowd or a public facilitates the development of new
forms of sociability albeit often of an ephemeral kind, for
the old stable and traditional forms are, as it were,
melted down, in these groupings.

Mannheim also distinguishes between genuine social
groups and social classes. He defines the latter as social
layers composed of men in similar social positions, with
an equal chance of going through the same experiences
in a given society. There is a certain degree of proba-

[1] *Essays on Sociology and Social Psychology* (1953), Introduction, p. 5.

bility that similar expectations and life-experiences will induce people to develop similar patterns of feeling, thought and action. But whereas men who find themselves in identical class situations might or might not develop a community of feeling and action; in the case of genuine social groups such a community of response is a condition of the existence of the group.

The question, why does man behave differently in the frame-work of the different social groups, and class-situations, is one of the fundamental problems which Mannheim attempts to answer. He believes that the various patterns of behaviour, thought and feeling of group members correspond to the type of integration represented by the group in question. Consequently, the analysis of the various types of integration and the classification of the different social groups is of fundamental importance. Mannheim emphasises that the principle of classification chosen by the sociologist must differ greatly from that chosen by the statistician. The latter, in need of measurable units, prefers to choose external group characteristics under such headings as age, sex, income, residence, etc. Such statistical groups, however, usually include a number of people who are united only in the mind of the statistician. The sociologist, on the other hand, has usually, in Mannheim's opinion, to find concepts which define genuine social groups, the members of which are integrated in social life through real, and more or less stable relationships. He asserts that purely external characteristics rarely form real links between people, whereas the bonds which create constant social relationships are mostly 'psychological' and 'spiritual'. He claims that such social links exercise a definite influence upon human behaviour, and that their effect could be recognised and analysed by anybody trained to use the tools of sociological research. This empirical character of the groups which are constituted by social links, is coupled in Mannheim's sociology with the psychological and spiritual character of the link itself. By stressing the specifically human and spiritual character of the links which create a community of feeling and action among men, Mannheim bars the way to the naturalistic and deterministic explanations of social phenomena as can be seen in the chapter in which he gives a critical appraisal of the Marxian theory of social change. We are, equally, a long way away from the various positivistic and naturalistic sociologies which claimed that man and society should be studied as if these were nothing but parts of external nature, and that the methods of sociological investigation should be similar to those applied in the natural sciences.

Mannheim delegates the study of the impact of external factors, such as natural environment, upon social life to the specialised 'auxiliary' disciplines, human geography or demography. He claims that it is the analysis of the results of human interactions which constitutes the real subject matter of analytic sociology. He realises that situations may arise when the external factors, as studied by the statistician or geographer, might 'correspond' to real social bonds. This might happen, for example, in the case of certain linguistic groups or income brackets. Yet, even in these instances the methods used by the statistician cannot furnish an answer to the question whether the external factors have or have not turned into a genuinely uniting force between men. Economic or linguistic factors can become socially relevant group-forming links only if they are regarded by a sufficient number of men and women as playing a vital part in their life.

By stressing the internal, psychic character of social bonds, Mannheim leads us towards a deeper understanding of social life. He stresses that in order to be effective all factors which link people in society must become constituent parts of the inner world of interacting persons through the mechanism of identification: secondly, that the group-forming factors are integral parts of a wider social process. Consequently, the sociologist has to utilise the analytic tools of a dynamic psychology as well as a systematic theory of society, and cannot rely upon quantitative methods or pure common sense. Mannheim's principle of group classification is in harmony with this theory.

Although Mannheim's analysis dissolves the group into its constituent elements, he denies that these elements are isolated and self-sufficient individuals. He analyses the social groups as the resultants of different social forces and processes, and although these processes are in fact different forms of interaction between individuals they cannot be deduced from the deliberate, conscious decisions and purposes of single individuals. Having a structural character and being the constituent parts of a dynamic society, these forces and processes must be analysed and compared with one another within the frame-work of a systematic theory of society.

Mannheim begins his systematic investigation of social life with a description of the elementary processes which are found in most societies (see Part Two). According to him the elementary social processes differ from the social phenomena of 'Great Society', such as institutions and stratification. They belong to the minutiae of society and their importance lies in the fact that they take part in directly shaping the individual. When analysing the various group-forming processes he follows in the footsteps of the pioneer of the German school of formal sociology, Georg Simmel, and of the American sociologist, Charles H. Cooley. But Mannheim goes one step further than his predecessors by applying the analytic tools of modern dynamic psychology. He investigates the psychological aspects of the intimate and frequent contacts within primary groups, such as the family, friendship groups or school classes which lead to the 'introjection of the impulses and sentiments' prevailing in such relationships. This psychological mechanism explains the fact that primary groups play such an important part in the shaping of the emotions, views and behaviour of man. Mannheim stresses that it is in these groups that the identification with others is first experienced by the growing person, and it is here that the feeling of social unity first emerges. Such capacity for identification normally returns later in life on a larger scale in the so-called secondary contact groups, like the church, the political party, the nation or the state. Mannheim shows here a keen interest in the problem of the transfer of emotions from the private to the public sphere, a problem which also fascinated Lasswell during the same period.

Beginning with the most simple and elementary social processes Mannheim proceeds with a step by step analysis of processes of increasing complexity. At each stage he contrasts the antithetical, yet complementary, processes. Thus, creating social contact is contrasted with creating social distance in society; the process of socialisation is compared with the individualisation of personalities. The various forms of struggle and social competition are set against the process of monopolisation on the one hand and co-operation on the other. He shows also that these processes are intimately linked with the different forms of social selection. Finally, Mannheim analyses the importance of the division of labour, and stresses the fact that this is one of the strongest integrating forces in modern society. He repeatedly points to the historical role played by the economic needs which induce men to co-operate systematically with each other and to set up permanent systems of integration. Yet he is not a defender of historical materialism and emphasises the importance of the non-economic factors in history and society. According to him, men co-operate to create stronger systems of military defence, more efficient forms of administration, but religious worship must also be considered as a focus of social integration.

By analysing the life and phenomena of society in terms of integrating and individualising processes, Mannheim encounters the following complication: elementary social processes affect not only the individual, the member of a group, but also the groups themselves. The integrating and separating forces act on two planes: firstly, within the groups, and secondly, between the groups, in the framework of 'Great Society'. The advantage of this view is that it enables us to analyse the structure of complex, modern society in terms of group relationships, subject to elementary social processes. Great Society is conceived by Mannheim as a society of groups, subject to largely the same forces and processes as the individual. The State is defined by Mannheim as the frame group of modern society, a special group which organises and regulates the relationship between the groups which constitute society.

In this group analysis of society and politics Mannheim goes even a step further when he raises the problem of international relations in terms of social processes which take place between conflicting and co-operating frame groups, the modern states. While outlining the conditions of setting up an effective international authority he draws our attention to the fact that mankind has not yet succeeded in setting up such a frame group to ensure co-operation between states and the peaceful solution of international conflicts.

The concluding chapters of the third part of this book, which deal with the dynamics of political groups, the sociology of classes and with a definition of the modern state, form a fascinating introduction to the basic problems of political sociology.

In Part Four ('Social Stability and Social Change') Mannheim turns to the problems of social structure and starts with the study of some of those forces which make for social cohesion and stability. According to him, social control is the sum of those methods by which society influences human behaviour in order to maintain a given order. Among a multitude of social controls, Mannheim picks out the most important ones such as custom and law, and analyses these both in isolation and also as mutually depending upon each other. He shows the displacement of custom by law, but also the new functions of customs in modern society.

He then undertakes a further step by describing the personal representatives of social control, the man in authority. This leads to an analysis of the situations in which leadership emerges, as well as to a sociological examination of prestige. Authority and prestige imply valuations and therefore Mannheim feels induced to conclude his analysis of social controls with a sociology of valuations. This is perhaps one of the most original and fascinating chapters of the book as Mannheim here applies the technique of analysis which he developed in his various contributions to the sociology of knowledge.

In the last chapter of this book Mannheim discusses the problem of the deeper causes of social change. He starts with an analysis of the Marxist theory of social change, 'historical materialism', and attempts to point out both the positive contributions of the theory to our knowledge of the mainsprings of social change and also the limitations of this theory. This is not the only place in this book where Mannheim, as we have seen, tries to overcome the limitations inherent in a purely economic interpretation of social and cultural dynamics.

The question arises whether Mannheim really succeeded in overcoming the limitations of a materialistic outlook or whether he only replaced 'economic determinism' by a less crude 'sociological determinism'. Only an analysis of the method applied by Mannheim in these lectures as well as a review of his ultimate aims as a sociologist can yield an answer to this question, and to these two questions we now turn.

The Method of Systematic Sociology

Mannheim's theory of man and society, as presented in this book, is full of contradictions and antithetical notions. This may be regarded as a re-emergence, as an attempt at a more general synthesis, of the dialectical views on culture which were characteristic of his early philosophical work. The synthesis is more general in the sense that Mannheim, during his London years, sought to weld together the speculative and empirical methods. The supporters of a rigidly empirical philosophy might question whether a synthesis between the speculative and empirical methods is possible or even desirable in the realm of the social sciences. Mannheim's results seem to show that the application of such a synthetic method can be fruitful and at the same time enables the scholar to avoid those pitfalls which, according to the spokesmen of the extreme empiricist school, are unavoidable, once the door is open to speculative methods. Mannheim was aware of the fact that theorising about the meaning of events would be empty talk without a specific and intimate knowledge of the always changing social realities, and urged that sociological interpretations and theories should be constantly checked in the light of practical experiences. Like Max Weber, he consequently rejected the claims of the intuitionists and the supporters of the morphological assessment as these showed little, if any, respect for empirical methods and renounced the quest for verifiable causal explanations. Further Mannheim emphatically rejects the notion that social groups and institutions should be regarded as substantial units or mythical entities. He demands that the sociologist should be trained to analyse groups and other social relationships, regarded by many as mythical entities, as products of social forces and processes. On the other hand Mannheim does not follow the opponents of the Platonist and Hegelian view in their extreme individualism and atomism. In fact, he fought a two-front war on the one hand against the neo-Hegelians and morphologists of his time, such as Oswald Spengler, Othmar Spann and Hans Freyer, and on the other against extreme empiricists and individualists such as Bertrand Russell or F. A. Hayek. In this respect Mannheim can be regarded as a follower of Max Weber, who continually strove to improve upon Weber's procedure. The application of psychological analysis in the interpretation of social situations is one of Mannheim's most important contributions in this direction.[1]

In this book Mannheim tries to reach a genuine synthesis between the methods of modern dynamic psychology and those of sociology. As a sociologist he naturally stresses the role played by social factors in the forming of behaviour and thought patterns, and he claims that even the forms of individualisation originate in social processes. Yet, he takes into consideration not only the process of introjection of social situations into the psyche which itself is made up of interacting aspects of the self, but also the projection of inner tensions and mental concepts into the so-called external, social field. By analysing the role both of introjection and projection in the social process he escapes the one-sidedness of the extreme 'sociologistic' view, according to which it is the social situation alone which determines human development.

His description of the different processes which create social distance, such as the 'fear distance', the 'power distance' and the distance between different status groups, shows his virtuosity in fusing external, 'situational' and internal 'psychological' factors in the analysis

---

[1] In the original plan of the course of lectures on which a large part of this book is based, Mannheim had included a lecture on 'Causality, Function and Structure Dialectics'. It was not in fact given, but in it he intended to show that social structures correspond to the network of interaction of single causes. He wrote on this topic in *Essays on the Sociology of Culture* (pp. 59–81) and Ernest Mannheim comments on it in his editorial introduction to that book.

of social and cultural phenomena. Another example of this can be found in his analysis of situations favouring the emergence of tyrannical rulers. He points out that specific forms of social and economic organisation and power distribution must coincide with certain cultural and psychic processes in order that a political leader should be permitted to turn into a tyrant, an isolated and domineering figure who, without incurring ridicule or revenge, can indulge in narcissistic notions of all-powerfulness and in orgies of self-glorification.

The weighing of the various factors of social and cultural development and the rejection of any single-cause theory recalls the procedure of Max Weber who analysed a multiplicity of causal factors, such as the control of the physical means of coercion, and of administration, the ownership of economic goods, the development of science as well as of religious and ethical attitudes, when investigating the rise of economic and political structures and institutions. Yet, there is a significant difference between Weber and Mannheim. In Max Weber's system the relationship between the various factors is a much looser one, and their co-existence in a given situation seems incidental; he proceeds, as if believing in the rule of 'chance' in history. Mannheim, however, sees the various factors of social evolution as active within an all-embracing social and cultural process. He perceives the basic unity in the development of society, without losing sight of the various aspects of culture and the peculiarities of human activities. His procedure is characterised by a sort of speculative boldness which distinguishes his method from the pragmatism of Weber. The roots of this difference can be found in Mannheim's training in the application of a speculative, dialectical logic and his ceaseless search for synthesis and integration.

Anyone who has tried to think in this way can appreciate that what Mannheim has to say is not just intelligent sociologising, but interpretation based upon a massive knowledge. His attempts to reconcile apparently contradictory methods of research culminate in a *tour de force*: he applies both the generalising and the individualising method, resolving their conflict by allotting to each method different tasks in the various spheres of sociology. According to Mannheim, the study of elementary social processes and the study of social groups is most appropriate for the generalising and formal method. However, such phenomena of Great Society as social stratification and institutions of a given society can be best studied by applying the individualising or historical method. The formal generalising method should be applied in the study of social phenomena which are characteristic of *all* societies, whilst the structure of concrete societies succeeding each other in history should be analysed sociologically with the help of the individualising method. By this procedure Mannheim hoped to solve the conflict between those who wished to propound principles common to any society, and those who wished, following the historical method, to expose the principles characteristic of specific societies. This clash of aim and method had divided the social scientists of the Continent into two hostile camps ever since the romantic and historical reaction against the spirit of the 'enlightenment' had first begun to appear. Mannheim believed that he could reconcile the two approaches.

Although realising the usefulness of a formal and generalising method in the analysis of the recurrent phenomena of social life, Mannheim never accepted the thesis that a generalising method, akin to those of the natural sciences, should be applied to the study of social and cultural life. He disregarded the attempt to transform social facts, that is meaningful human relationships, into measurable quantities in order to study them as if they were physico-chemical processes. He was convinced that social and cultural processes have their own peculiar dynamics which cannot be studied with the help of the same methods as physico-chemical, or even biological processes.

In this book Mannheim applies mostly a generalising method, but adapts it to his subject. He claims that general sociology should deal systematically with such social phenomena as are characteristic of all societies. These are the so-called minutiae of social life which shape the individual and act as intimate links between the members of a group. Although Mannheim begins these lectures by emphasising the need for a study of the minutiae of social life, he is soon compelled to draw into the web of his analysis such phenomena of Great Society as authoritarian and democratic power structures, urbanisation and industrialisation, the modern state. He examines these and other phenomena of Great Society (like social classes and forces of social control and social change) by following a generalising method, but occasionally he refers to results which were obtained in other branches of sociology with the aid of historical and individualising methods.

Having considered the method appropriate to systematic sociology, it has become apparent that there are other questions of aims and assumptions implicit in the method which we should examine.

The Ultimate Aims of the Sociologist

Mannheim, when advocating the use of different methods of research, reminds his readers of the dangers of 'eclecticism' but claims that a real synthesis between the various methods hitherto applied in the different branches of the social sciences is possible. This optimism is based on his conviction that the sociologist is pre-eminently fitted to synthesise the results of the specialised social sciences which deal with the different aspects of human culture and society. The speculative philosophers of the nineteenth century had already attempted to break through the walls of specialisation and to create a central discipline dealing with the problems of man, but they did not realise that it was necessary to provide broad empirical foundations for such a discipline. Mannheim believed that twentieth-century sociology could succeed where nineteenth-century philosophy had failed. He might have been over-confident as to the great future tasks and achievements of the sociologist, but his virtuosity in the use of the various methods of social and cultural analysis cannot be denied.

Yet, in following Mannheim's argument the critic might feel that something valuable has been lost. The clear outlines of the picture of man and society, as constructed by scholars with a narrower but more coherent outlook, had to be sacrificed for the sake of inclusiveness. When denying the domination of a single factor over social and cultural evolution, the sociologist might lose, as it were, a key to some understanding of history and society. It seems that even to-day the attraction of simplified pictures of human evolution is considerable. This attraction might be explained by the fact that in the modern crisis man requires an interpretation of history which can serve as a guide for action in an otherwise obscure and disconcerting social situation. However, Mannheim also hoped that a true science of man and society could supply us with a guide for action and would function as a compass showing the way towards a better society and a more meaningful life. Yet he denied the virtues of simplification and believed that only a more comprehensive knowledge of man, even if it was at present necessarily vague, could lead to real progress both in the field of theoretical knowledge and in that of practical action.

Since the collapse of the Weimar Republic he incessantly studied the question: how could the sociologist contribute to a solution of the modern social and cultural crisis? In his theoretical work he tried to detect those economic, social, political and psychological determinants which, if correctly handled, would enable the social reformer to influence human development. The scientist's quest for hidden structural connections between the different spheres of man's activities was complemented by the moral reformer's search for the principles of social and cultural reconstruction. During his London years Mannheim's work as a social scientist shows increasingly active characteristics and he moved far away from the relativism and detachment amounting almost to fatalism which had dominated his outlook at the time of the Weimar Republic. His plans for social reform were always based upon sociological insight, as he never believed in the power of pure ideas and goodwill. He remained convinced that a comprehensive knowledge of all social factors was absolutely necessary. He believed that a sociologically trained educationalist and social administrator would be more likely to succeed where those who relied only on goodwill and on abstract principles had failed.

As a result, Mannheim's theoretical sociology is not a fatalistic one, nor are his suggestions of social reform, as they developed particularly in his later books, utopian in character. Already in this mainly theoretical work representing his earliest teaching after his arrival in England, the careful reader can detect the author's interest in the burning issues which were to be central in his later works dealing with the problems of social reconstruction and planning for freedom. In fact, the book which follows contains the theoretical and analytical spade work which prepared the field for his call to practical reform.

Those who believe that man is guided by 'enlightened reason', 'economic self-interest', 'biological instincts', or 'faith' alone, will repudiate Mannheim's claim that his complex theory could serve as the basis for a guide for social action. But if the motives of men are mixed, then a broadly based and inclusive theory of human behaviour and social development such as this is should furnish some opportunity of forming a reliable theoretical basis for social and cultural reform.

J. S. ERÖS
W. A. C. STEWART

Keele,
June, 1957

SYSTEMATIC SOCIOLOGY

Introduction

The Scope of Sociology and of the Social Sciences

In the book which follows I have not covered the whole field of the social sciences, nor even the whole field of sociology. It would be wise at this point to give at least a survey of the whole field.

By the term 'social sciences' we understand, in contradistinction to the natural sciences, all those scientific disciplines which deal with man, not so much as a part of nature but as a being who builds up societies and cultures. All knowledge which helps us to a better understanding of this social and cultural process is either a part of or an auxiliary discipline to the social sciences.

In this largest sense of the word all the cultural sciences belong to the field of the social sciences; for instance, philology, the history of literature, the history of art, the history of knowledge, economics, economic history, political science and anthropology. But this huge amount of material must be formed into some coherence by a central discipline which has both a point of view and a subject matter of its own. In the field of social sciences the central discipline is *sociology*. It is on the one hand a synthetic discipline, trying to unify from a central point of view the results of the separate disciplines; and it is on the other hand an analytic and specialised discipline with its own field of research. The specialised subject matter of sociology is the forms of living together of man, the sum of which we call society.

I shall consider some of the main forms of this living together, such as social contacts, social distance, isolation, individualisation, co-operation, competition, division of labour and social integration. The forms of this living together can be described and explained on two lines and therefore we have two main sections of sociology:

Systematic and general sociology which describes one by one the main factors of this living together as far as they may be found in every kind of society. It is called general sociology because the general forms and tendencies, as they may be found in every society, primitive as well as modern, are to be described in it. It is called systematic sociology because it does not deal with these factors of the living together of man in a haphazard way but in a systematic order, following the line from the simplest to the most complex and settled forms of integration—from transitory contacts up to the frame-group.

Besides general sociology we have *historical sociology*. This part of sociology deals with the historical variety and actuality of these general forms. Historical sociology falls into two sections: firstly comparative sociology and secondly social dynamics. These are not my concern in the discussions which follow.

Comparative sociology considers a transition from general sociology to dynamic sociology. It deals mainly with the historical variations of the same phenomenon and tries to find by comparison general features which are to be separated from individual features. Comparative studies on such institutions as marriage, family, law, education or government belong here.

By *social dynamics* we understand an historical study of society which deals with the interrelations between the various social factors and institutions in a certain given society; for instance, a primitive tribe, or the society of ancient Rome, of modern England or of modern Europe. This kind of sociology presumes knowledge both of general and of comparative sociology but it is more concerned with the unique setting of the phenomena implied (for instance the Roman family or the modern family of a certain social stratum) and is mainly interested in the problem of how the working of one social unit reacts upon the other (for instance, how the life of the tribe interacts with the life and forms of behaviour of the family within it). This kind of sociology is called dynamic because it has not only to answer how one social institution or social factor reacts upon others at a given moment—looking at an artificially static cross-section of history—but has also to answer the question as to where the driving force is to be found which brings about changes in the social structure in a given society. Sometimes the main changes may be due to the transformation of the technique of production but sometimes a new kind of power organisation or some other innovation is the starting point of social transformation and the related cultural changes.

So historical and dynamic sociology are two principal modes of inquiry in the study of the subject. They try to explain the changing life of society. In the discussions which follow in this book, I am not, however, concerned with historical and dynamic sociology but with the main problems of systematic and general sociology—that is, with the main factors of living together in any kind of society.

In order to be able to examine social facts the elements of sociological analysis have to be acquired. This means that one must first be a sociologist in order to become a specialist in one sphere later, for instance in education or in social work. In order to establish these requirements, the sociologist should first analyse the *psychological equipment of man*. In order to obtain a correct picture of this equipment we have to analyse the relationship of instincts to habits, the transformation of emotions and of the libido and the nature of interests and attitudes. This kind of analysis of human behaviour enables us to understand that social facts are never what they seem to be. For instance, the psychological assumptions apparent in stereotypes of masculinity or femininity, as well as of social habits, are usually mistaken for instincts. Nor will

3

the untrained observer notice behind ideologies the social guidance of emotions.

Secondly, the student of society should consider *the most elementary social processes*, such as contacts, distance, social hierarchy, isolation, competition, conflict, cooperation, division of labour and personality formation, as producing both conformity and individualisation. Thirdly, all these psychological and social factors must be related to *the nature of social integration* analysing such integrations as the crowd, the group and the social classes.

These, then, are the first three parts of this book—man and his psychic endowment, elementary social processes and the nature of social integration. In the fourth part we go a step further to examine some of the factors which make for social stability and for social change.

PART 1

MAN AND HIS
PSYCHIC EQUIPMENT

CHAPTER I

Man and His Psychic Equipment

I do not wish to attempt here a treatise on the biology and psychology of man. I shall enumerate only those results of these disciplines which explain the fact that man is capable of being shaped by society. By itself living in society would not have such far-reaching consequences if man had not a fundamental quality which lower animals lack; that quality is the flexibility of his behaviour. Ants and bees also live together, they too have a kind of division of labour and a kind of state, but, unlike man, there is no visible change in their psychic life—they still reproduce the same social and mental patterns, and in that sense they have no history.

In order to understand fully this statement it is necessary to work out the meaning of some fundamental notions, such as behaviour, behaviour pattern, situation and adjustment.

1. BEHAVIOUR, SITUATION AND ADJUSTMENT

As an introduction I would like to give an example. If you are at a party where you do not know anybody, and furthermore where the members of the group are either on a higher level in the social scale than you or your family, or on a lower level, then you are likely to become shy and not be sure how to act. The same might happen to you if you join a party in a foreign country with whose customs you are not familiar. Shyness is a symptom of a

7

lack of adjustment to a new situation, and is a consequence of the fact that you do not know how to behave. In order to avoid this embarrassment either you look for a kind of behaviour which fits the new situation or you ask somebody how to behave. In the latter case you are prepared to accept a traditional behaviour pattern, in the former you try to invent a new behaviour pattern.

Of course animals also look for right behaviour if they meet physical obstacles and they make adjustments to a newly emerging situation. In fact, adjustment is the most elementary process underlying all our activities. A behaviour pattern is a definite relationship between a stimulus and response, which causes the organism to behave in a characteristic and uniform manner whenever the specific stimulus occurs. A behaviour pattern may be either instinctive and thus inherited, or habitual and acquired.

But what is the difference between the adjustment made by an animal and our adjustments in society? An animal adapts itself as a rule to situations arising from natural surroundings with a very small scale of variability. Man, besides adapting himself to his natural surroundings, adapts himself also to the psycho-social-institutional environment, with a large variety in the situations demanding flexible responses. Thus great variability of behaviour and adaptation to surroundings of a social character is typical for man.

The child comes into the world endowed with mechanisms of neural action involving muscular movement. Respiration, circulation and digestion are the first physiological functions he carries out. The first movements of his limbs are random and spontaneous, but he soon acquires the power of muscular co-ordination, and repetition causes useful movements to become automatic. As time passes, inherited and acquired reflexes (such as choking, coughing, trembling, sneezing or crying from pain) can, up to a point, be consciously modified.

8

Animals inherit the mental pattern which they need for the performance of the few tasks they have to fulfil, and a newly born animal shows a mastery over the most important behaviour patterns immediately after its birth. An infant, however, is born helpless, with very few fixed behaviour patterns. He needs a long breeding period during which he acquires the most important of these. He obtains them from society, which stores for the individual those patterns of adjustment necessary for life in that society. On the other hand man can, during his lifetime, change his behaviour patterns and find new ones by the method of trial and error or by other means. Animals make the trial-and-error adjustments too, by being physically engaged in the trials and errors while man can make his adjustment in his mind, by searching for the right action in thought. An animal, having made an adjustment to an unusual physical environment, does not remember as a rule the behaviour which has brought the bad and the good result, it cannot communicate its experiences to other animals and it can seldom co-operate in making adjustments with others. Man can think out with the help of imagination more possibilities of action in a few minutes than even the evolved type of animal could acquire by trial-an-error action over a long period of its life.

The main difference between lower animals and man is that animals adapt themselves to situations by inherited behaviour patterns which we call instincts, whilst man has not only those fixed instincts which are adequate to the tasks which his environment lays upon him, but is forced to acquire new behaviour patterns during his lifetime. He has been able to make such great progress during the course of history because the most significant forms of adjustment for him are transmitted by the psycho-social-institutional medium which we call our social and cultural life, and not by biological inheritance. Such biological inheritance would necessitate the

9

passage of thousands of years, before a fitting adjustment became a part of the inherited racial memory.

The main error of racial theories can be found in the assertion that culture is racially inherited. In fact culture is acquired in the lifetime of the individual and is passed on from one generation to another with the aid of such media as language and imitation. Institutions are nothing but forms of adjustment which have been fixed by tradition, and often reinforced by system, organisation, material features and possessions.

2. i. HABITS AND THE PROBLEM OF 'INSTINCTS'

Habits are behaviour patterns which are not the results of inheritance but the products of experience. Habit is relatively complex and is mostly built up of simple and almost instinctive behaviour patterns, the history of mankind being a continuous process of development of new habits arising out of new combinations of a few fundamental reflexes and simple instincts. This is the reason why we must study the simplest elements of human behaviour before we go further.

Habits which are really acquired behaviour patterns have been very often mistaken for instincts. The reason for such confusion is that habits which have been practised for some time by man become automatic. Many of the most fundamental habits are acquired in early childhood and the strenuous efforts which the individual undertook in learning them are likely to be forgotten. Hardly any psychologist or sociologist will now speak of the instinct of self-preservation or of the instinct of imitation, although on the other hand he sees many habits which may be described as tending towards self-preservation or as imitative. In the same way we have, on the whole, stopped speaking about the instincts of gregariousness, pugnacity, self-assertion, self-display or self-abasement, and we recognise such tendencies as habits. There is not, therefore, a democratic instinct, a criminal instinct, a political instinct, or an instinct of property. The earlier theory of fixed instinct had a socially conservative function. It served as a justification of tradition and superstition in social situations where new and better adjustments were needed. We believe to-day that changing situations demand new adjustments, new behaviour patterns and we know that man by his nature is capable of producing these.

Roughly speaking we can distinguish three main stages in the development of modern psychology. The first stage can be called that of intellectualism. James wrote in 1890 that nothing was more common among psychologists than the assertion that human life is governed by reason, while the lower animals are controlled by instincts. Twenty years later we find the second stage, when psychologists recognised the existence of a number of instincts in man and the problem was what the predisposing factors might be. By 1920 the serious attempts to secure fruitful results from varying lists of instincts had become so discouraging that doubt was cast on the theory itself. The way out from this impasse was found by such social psychologists as Dewey, Znaniecki, G. M. Williams and others. As Dewey has put it, 'The instincts do not make the institutions; it is the institutions that make the instincts.' The old units of behaviour patterns are in every new situation broken up and their elements are combined and are formed afresh in every specific readjustment. Dewey also wrote: 'We know that culture is neither in the blood nor in the germ-plasm and that race means nothing as compared with the experience and activities of the group we are to study.' G. M. Williams in his book *Our Rural Heritage* gives a detailed account of the established attitudes of farmers living in New York State and he derives these from the social experiences of groups of farmers. Znaniecki in his *Laws of Social Psychology* develops his leading idea that acts and experiences are the determining antecedents beyond which it is not profitable or even possible to seek any stable elements or absolutes.

Thus, to-day, instead of considering human life as governed either by reason or by instinct, the first two phases of development of modern psychology mentioned above, we speak of tendencies which come to be fixed by specific tasks presented by the changing situations. This is a dynamic concept of instincts, which leaves open the operation of social forces and actualities. As we shall see, it does not exclude the possibility of influence by unconscious aspects of experience.

ii. THE HABIT-MAKING MECHANISM

We have seen that behaviour patterns leading to good adjustments which become habitual are of the greatest importance to mankind, mainly because they save time and energy. However if the situations in which we act change fundamentally, nothing could be more disadvantageous than a rigid habit which does not fit in with new conditions. Since modern society is built up of a set of very rapidly changing situations, there is a great need to remake those of our adjustments which have become obsolete. For this reason we must turn our attention at this point to the problem of the habit-making mechanism.

Making behaviour patterns is accomplished through responses to stimuli, and new combinations of stimuli may bring about new combinations of responses. There are very simple stimuli which condition responses automatically. For instance, the hungry infant sucks instinctively, or the pupil of the eye contracts sharply in a bright light. In such cases we can speak of an instinctive response which is biologically adequate. That is the starting-point—but we have seen that human society is not constituted by responses to instinctive stimuli only.

There is a much larger range of possible responses than these.

What is the elementary mechanism which makes these more complex responses possible? The elementary mechanism, which creates responses that are not purely biological, is the conditioned, acquired reflex which was described for the first time by Pavlov. The experiments which Pavlov undertook with dogs have become famous. It was well known that hungry dogs normally respond to the presence of raw meat with a flow of saliva. In this case meat is an adequate biological stimulus provoking instinctive responses. Pavlov caused a bell to be rung a number of times simultaneously with the presentation of the meat. After a period of such training he experimented by ringing the bell without presenting the meat, with the result that the saliva of dogs exposed to the stimulus of the ringing bell only, flowed just the same. The bell, which was originally insufficient by itself to set off a response in dogs, acquired the power of conditioning the same reflex, which was formerly only conditioned by the biologically adequate stimulus, the presentation of meat.

Another experiment showing the same process can be made with bees: we put honey on red paper and a group of bees gets the habit of collecting the honey from the red paper. After a time the bees seek for honey on any red paper they notice, even if there is no honey on it. Similarly spiders to whom we have given flies to eat, previously plunged into turpentine, will in future show reluctance to catch any flies.

These simple experiments exemplify that elementary process which assists the creation of social life in general —the process of responses answering to stimuli which are not simply biologically adequate, as for instance when we learn to like foods which our parents like or if we learn to approve the religious and political views which they approve. In such cases we accept through sympathy conditioned responses which originally were not connected

13

with the stimulus. In this way we may gradually take over most of the attitudes of those with whom we associate closely. If we blush when somebody says anything 'shocking' in conversation, this is the result of the fact that we were brought up in surroundings where the mentioning of such things was accompanied by appalled silence on the part of parents, teachers and others, so that we cannot hear these words without recapturing the painful emotions aroused in us during childhood. Education in the widest sense leans heavily on this kind of associated response.

It was the French sociologist Tarde who stressed very strongly the social role of the process of imitation. Imitation is a conditioned reflex, but it is not similar to the elementary process outlined above. It is a kind of system of combined conditioned responses. Imitation is the method by which the cultural content of society is transmitted from one generation to another. In the case of imitation it is the behaviour of another which is the efficient conditioning stimulus to the same behaviour in ourselves.

Thus we can distinguish two kinds of responses to stimuli: those made by ourselves as a consequence of our own experiences, and those which are accepted by imitation. In the second case we take someone as our model and learn to do as he does. For instance we take as our models people who have prestige, because we think that there is a functional relationship between their behaviour and their success.

3. EVOLUTION IN THE MODELS OF IMITATION

There is an evolution in the child's life from the more concrete to the more abstract forms of behaviour, and from proximate personalities to more distant ones. The child begins by imitating his mother or nurse, and later adds such models as the father, brothers and sisters, playmates and teachers, impressive figures like the postman or the members of the gang which he has joined. The first type of imitation takes as models the simpler acts and emotions of those persons near to the child. As the range of experience widens the process of imitation gradually becomes more extensive, more fundamental and more abstract. During the early teens there is a gradual transition from concrete personality models to ideal ones. For instance the personalities described in the stories which we tell children or which are presented to them in biographies, can be valuable assets in the process of influencing and integrating personality-responses. The danger of such models is that the sense of reality is absent. The disproportion in modern man's life sometimes becomes very painful. The small range of experiences afforded by the specialised work of a certain occupation or by narrow surroundings is often in blatant contradiction to the information and impressions which we obtain from newspapers, books and the cinema. Such a disproportion can help to produce a somewhat unbalanced personality, who possesses acquired behaviour patterns which neither correspond to the character and status of the person in question, nor to the field of his real activity. The danger for many intellectuals consists in the possibility that they may think and behave quite differently, without noticing consciously the discrepancy, or, more seriously, while noticing the discrepancy and experiencing only a crippling frustration thereby.

4. SOCIOLOGICAL AND PSYCHOANALYTIC DESCRIPTIONS OF MAN

When we were considering conditioned reflexes we raised the question of the relationship between the conditioning of reflexes and society. Man in society experiences the interplay of complex internal and external pressures, and his reaction to these has both an individual and a social significance. If we described society without previously analysing the psychic equipment and the mental forces of man, we would make the same mistake as a man who attempted to describe an electric motor without any knowledge of the nature and working of electric power. But if we limited ourselves to giving an account of the nature of the psychic energies of the individual, we would be acting like a man who explained the nature of electric power without giving a description of the machine which it drives, or the work it can be expected to do.

I started my analysis by outlining some of the most important notions of the behaviouristic approach in psychology. I now wish to consider some of the important ideas in Freudian psychology, selecting those notions which are necessary for a satisfactory explanation of the working of society. I am neither a behaviourist, nor a Freudian, nor a Marxist. Each of these schools, in my view, presents a partial analysis, while seeming to establish a whole system. I am trying to use the result of the investigations of all three, to obtain a more adequate picture of the working of society.

There is an essential difference between the Freudian and the behaviouristic approaches. The behaviouristic approach is entirely externalised, because for behaviourists it is overt behaviour that counts. The only accepted data are movements and bodily changes. Inner observation, introspection, sympathetic intuition are called by the behaviourist 'metaphysical' and are rejected. As a consequence he reduces the facts of consciousness to facts of overt behaviour. Behaviourism is furthermore entirely mechanistic. Reactions are always connected to stimuli, they are independent of the total personality and the personality is not a unitary configuration, but a mosaic-like agglomeration of reactions. On the other hand, the fruitful elements in behaviourism are to be found in the fact that there are partial and isolated mechanisms in animals and in man which are automatic and are independent of the personality.

Man's psychic equipment and his social character cannot be wholly defined in terms of behaviour patterns, habits, adjustments, imitations and ideologies. The development of a personality does not consist only in the process of conditioning new responses. The mechanical laws of association are not sufficient for the interpretation of man.

We must build into the pragmatist and behaviourist concept of man's psychology some fundamental notions worked out by psychoanalysts, without becoming totally committed to the Freudian view. These fundamental notions are: the unconscious, repression, and sublimation.

i. REPRESSION

When man makes his vital adjustments, such as co-operating with his fellow-men in society or doing his daily work, he disposes of psychic energy. In the process he uses and adapts forces called drives, which were originally striving to fulfil the elementary needs of the organism, such as self-preservation and procreation. Both create impulses and wishes which strive for fulfilment and this has to be achieved in a social situation. Every real adjustment seems to be connected negatively with the repression of those quantities of energy which cannot be used in the social situation, and positively with the 'selection' of appropriate behaviour and states of mind and attitude. We mostly repress those impulses and the ideas connected with them, which are banned by society. The so-called 'censor' in personality structure postulated by the Freudians, is mostly composed of inhibitions which have been reinforced by living in society. Repression is one of the defence techniques the individual uses to protect his conscious life against wishes which could cause painful conflicts in his consciousness. That is to say we repress mainly those strivings which could not reach their goal in a given society. Primal repression refers to material which was never conscious, the so-called archaic repressions. Repression proper expels into the unconscious material which has been conscious or pre-conscious.

All our physical wishes, and those which derive from them, cannot be fulfilled at will, so repression is a normal process which accompanies every kind of response to given stimuli. It compels the individual at every moment to renounce the fulfilment of some of his wishes by apparently selecting others which he is usually satisfied at having chosen. On the other hand these drives and wishes, although repressed, still strive for satisfaction. Even systematic logical thought is built up upon a series of repressions. We always repress certain associations in order to attain a given end. Lasswell asserts that a careful scrutiny of individual behaviour over a twenty-four-hour period strikingly shows the extent to which the personality is controlled by very elementary psychological structures. Much of the energy of the personality is spent on blocking the entry of the maladjusted impulses of the self into consciousness and into overt responses.

According to Freud the repressed drive, the repressed energy, continues to work in our unconscious. The aim of repressions is to keep out of consciousness impulses which are repugnant to the moral standards of society. The process of repression, similarly to the process of imitation, is normally a time-and-energy saving mechanism which spares our conscious life from dealing again and again with tendencies and wishes which cannot be fulfilled in a given social situation, or which would raise a long series of inner and external conflicts which could in the end threaten the existence of the individual.

Although I acknowledge the permanent necessity of the existence of certain repressive mechanisms, I claim that the better a social organism works, the less repression it needs. Society can help its members to adjust themselves by furnishing outlets and channels for the superfluous energies of individuals.

In order to understand these assertions of the Freudian school, it is necessary to know what kinds of typical expression the repressed energies may take. The repressed drive can be either completely repressed or remain partly unrepressed. In the latter case it will try to find an indirect expression. Completely repressed drives will not at this point constitute a problem for us, but a problem is presented by those drives which have not been wholly repressed.

ii. NEUROSIS, REACTION FORMATION AND PROJECTION

The first outlet for a not quite adjusted repression is the so-called *neurosis*. This is a partial solution of a psychological dilemma. The well-known example is war neurosis. Some soldiers during wartime were tormented by the following conflict: either to rush into battle, in which case the fear and anxiety of death or mutilation terrified them, at any rate for a time; or to stay out of such danger, which produced the fear of being considered by others as cowards. An accidental wound provides a way out from the painful conflict. In the absence of such an accident some soldiers unconsciously developed such symptoms as blindness or paralysis, they sought refuge in illness. Such paralysis or blindness being of a purely psychic origin might be cured by analysis or hypnosis.

These are admittedly pathological symptoms of maladjustment in the process of repression, but similar kinds of maladjustment are working in the more normal processes of society, as, for example, in the extravagant behaviour of some adolescents, in hero worship, or in the passionate behaviour of many crowds at sporting events.

Another way of dealing with weak or inadequate repressions is by *reaction formation*. Prudery of a militant kind is very often nothing but the expression of the hidden wish to have some kind of concern with sexual matters. Many people who display a hostile interest in the sexual problems of others, do so in order to distract attention from their own hidden wishes and attempt in this way to strengthen their repressions. The whole development of over-strict moral codes can only be explained by this mechanism of reaction formation.

Another technique is called *projection*. We tend to project our thoughts and emotions on to others and criticise them for these unmercifully. In this way a forbidden stimulus—experienced as an inner enemy—is projected on the outer world. An example is to be found when we project our own unconscious doubts about our love for a person or of our fidelity to our partner on to that partner in expressions of distrust and jealousy. Doubt and jealousy may thus very often be a result of projection. These typical processes on a level of lesser intensity may be found in many people, and the mechanism has to be studied by us if we want to understand the typical origin of hatred by projection. We know that savages people the external world with evil spirits, but this technique is a well-known phenomenon of twentieth-century Europe as well.

iii. RATIONALISATION

Rationalisation is another way of escaping conflicts. We speak of rationalisation if we impute other motives for our own conduct than those which have really moved us. Its essence is the construction of an explanation which is more a justification of our acts than a real account of the motivation for them. This method is employed usually if there are conflicts between our habits of acting and our standards of conduct, and a person either tells a lie consciously, or succeeds in deceiving himself by some explanation satisfying to himself while evading the real issue. This happens if people do things which are out of harmony with their conscious standards, but by giving another reason for their deeds, they do not allow the discrepancies to disturb them any more.

Rationalisations are mostly used by people who live in two different, mutually incompatible environments. For instance, a child who was taught to be obedient to his parents and to be frank with them about everything he does, may come under the influence of a group of playmates who have elaborated a moral code quite different from that of the family. Consequently there will arise a conflict between 'gang behaviour' and 'family behaviour'. This leads to confusion of attitude and may lead towards repression. Much will be allowed in the gang that is forbidden in the family. There are three typical ways of reacting to this conflict. The first is by forgetting—the child speaking with his parents will really forget the behaviour which was disapproved of by his parents, and tell them what he has been doing, remembering his mistake too late. The second is by lying. The lies of small children should not be moralised about—they are often a symptom of a conflict. The third reaction is to rationalise. The child might try to justify his deeds by referring to the sanction of another authority—his teachers, 'what other people do', what the parents of other children let them do.

iv. SYMBOLISATION AND DAYDREAMING

The creation of symbols is yet a further way by which the human mind tries to find a discharge for repressed energies. A symbol helps us to obtain a fancied fulfilment of our wishes. We deceive ourselves by finding substitutes for our forbidden wants. By disguising, with the help of symbols, the real object of our wants we may be occupied in a hidden, latent way with it.

In this process of creating symbols, one object comes to represent another either by association or similarity, or by contrast. Mythology can be regarded as the system of primary symbols of humanity.

The role of symbols in political life is very great. Here collective symbols help the individual to overcome his private maladjustments. Lasswell has pointed out that political symbols like the flag, the monarchy, the proletariat, the fifth column, serve as targets for displaced personal emotional response. They are adapted to this because they are ambiguous and because they have a general circulation. The individual, says Lasswell, so to say, socialises his bodily symptoms and private obsessions 'by means of collective symbols in mass movements'.

Our dreams are full of symbols which, according to Freud, mostly represent wish-fulfilments which our conception of life would never permit. But even in our daily life we have periods when we lessen the strength of self-control and give an outlet to repressed experience or try to evade a difficult conflict. The essence of daydreaming is always the fanciful creation of a world that is more colourful, more appreciative of ourselves or in which our personality has a greater opportunity to be active, than is possible in our immediate surroundings. For instance, some children who are beginning to develop wants and desires, which cannot be adequately satisfied in their environment, react either by running away and seeking adventures elsewhere (these are the active types) or they turn inwards and seek to perform in their daydreaming a substitute for an unsatisfying reality. In both cases we see a manifestation of the expanding desire of the child for wider experiences and for new models of behaviour. Very often in such infantile situations the lineaments of future character formation in the individual appear. Once the child gets into the habit of solving his life conflicts by turning inwards, he becomes what is called an introverted personality. The active child finds new behaviour patterns to settle conflicts in changing his surroundings and adjusting himself to a real situation and may become an extravert personality.

Daydreaming is to a certain extent a helpful adjustment because it gives an outlet for energies by inducing the ego to tolerate what Healy calls 'fantasies of gratification' of an egoistic or of an erotic character. But if exaggerated, daydreaming may become an impediment to adjustments to real situations. The chronic daydreamer substitutes the easier method of imaginative achievements for the actual effort and realisation in the real world. Healy says of the daydreaming habit that in this case 'satisfaction is obtained entirely in a mental state'. He thinks that a growing individual should gradually bring the life of fantasy 'into closer relation with the facts of reality'. But he admits that fantasy is also 'a safety valve for the abreaction of strong affects'.

Daydreaming is correlated to the social situation where a large amount of leisure and a small range of activity compel the individual to use his superfluous energies in that way. Types whose activities do not absorb most of their energies, or people who work much but in a monotonous way, are predisposed to daydreaming; for instance, young girls, housewives who for various reasons are not absorbed by the duties of the household, employees in work which may have slack periods in the day, such as serving in shops, those in repetitive factory work, or wealthy idlers.

The cinema can be considered as a daydream-producing machine on the basis of large-scale industry. Modern mass-society produces more and more human beings with a very narrow scale of possibilities. They need a compensation and a substitute for lost activities—an outlet for their imagination. Formerly it was mainly the task of poetry, of the novel and of the theatre to give expression to these daydreaming tendencies. In earlier ages there were myths which had the same function. Psychoanalysts like Freud and Sachs have made comparisons between fantasy formation and artistic creation. The similarity can be found in the fact that both are free from the condition of reality, that both offer compensation for deficiencies and frustrations and both concern themselves frequently with pain, tragedy and happiness. The main difference—as Sachs has pointed out—is that the principal personage in a daydream is the self and it has a meaning only for the self, whereas the creations of art must have meaning for many. Further, daydreams are formless and without coherence except in terms of an individual's needs or wishes, whereas works of art must have form, unity and clarity.

V. SUBLIMATION AND IDEALISATION AND THEIR SOCIAL SIGNIFICANCE

There is much similarity between daydreaming and the process of idealisation and sublimation. The main difference is that in the latter case the superfluous emotional energy or libido is not used to create a second world besides the existing reality, but is used to spiritualise parts of real surroundings, to heighten the significance of real bits of environment. For instance, emotional energies of an erotic origin can be used—after having been transferred from their sexual origin—to idealise and spiritualise various persons and objects of our surroundings, such as the loved personality of the King or the Queen, of the political, religious or educational leader-personality, or the symbol of the fatherland, the party or the class.

Sublimation is a process that concerns the redirection of impulse, as when an earlier love of self-display becomes a generalised pleasure in achieving prominence in some career or calling. Idealisation concentrates upon the object and it represents a shift from the ego to the ego-ideal with the uncritical approbation which that implies. In the latter case the uncritical attitude refers to the object; in the former case, one is uncritical of oneself as one was in early childhood, in the period of feeling almighty. In psychoanalytic terms idealisation represents a displacement of early childhood self-love on to the superego and this process usually becomes particularly apparent during puberty.

The sociologist must note the importance, for personal and social integration, of the process of creating an ego-ideal. It offers a key to the way in which society, apart from the conditioning or encouragement of habits, can influence people. In fact, the ego-ideal is more important to the personality than all habit patterns, because habits and action patterns all become co-ordinated in the ego-ideal. This is the psychological side of the process. On the sociological side we see a point at which society can influence personality by means of ideas, myths, novels, and, of course, by religion.

Such social psychologists and sociologists as Emile Durkheim, Max Weber, G. H. Mead, J. F. Dashiell, M. Ginsberg and S. C. Pepper—to mention only a few— have stressed the importance of ideals in human society. According to Mead, social habits and customs are intimately connected with values. But values depend on social function. According to Pepper, human society is 'built around ideals'. Whilst societies co-operate in the service of certain purposes, 'these purposes are nothing other than ideals . . . ideals that actually function in morality. But for an ideal to function in morality, it must be more than a mere ideal. There must be co-operation of individuals about it, and that co-operation must be in some degree crystallised into a social structure. It is the action of the social structure that makes the obligation categorical. Until an ideal takes root in a social structure it can claim nothing, but hypothetical obligation. . . .'

Sloops again stresses the fact that ideals do not die when they are temporarily inhibited by the facts of the real world, which is unsympathetic to these ideas. Ideals, which are supported by love and by deeper instincts, but which are inhibited temporarily and deprived of expression in the objective world 'are forced down into the

25

deeper unconscious levels of the mind'. If the hostility of the real world continues, the deeper self will use the intellect to 'transform the suppressed ideal into some form of dream, some form of imagery, in which it can survive temporary defeat'. The ideal of righteous social order, for instance, took, in the Hellenistic period of Attic civilisation, the form of inner life. Christianity transformed this ideal into an inner life in which God and man communicated in both immanent and transcendent experience.

The social function of ideals is different in different phases of psychic and social organisation. In the individual phase, the concept of a mutually helpful society becomes charged with emotional content, but it is ineffectual if kept within individuals. In the collective or social phase an ideal-concept and the emotion connected with it become the basis for action and interaction within groups. Finally, in the institutional phase the forms of the interaction remain, but are no longer charged with emotion because the embodied ideal works, so to say, by itself. This is a notion explored by G. W. Allport in relation to the part played by instincts in the development of human personality. He calls the process of detachment from emotional roots and the resultant operating of an ideal 'functional autonomy'.

This is the way in which new reality is created. Emotions are needed only when institutions are lacking. The breaking of an old habit and the establishing of a new one needs emotion—this is the social function of emotion. Consequently, if the founder of a religious or other emotionally charged social movement wants to preserve the original emotional content of the movement, he must be hostile to institutionalisation, as institutions and the rational doctrines they need may tend to kill the enthusiasm of the faith.

CHAPTER II

Man and His Psychic Equipment
(continued)

5. THE SOCIAL GUIDANCE OF PSYCHIC
ENERGIES

Art, literature and all kinds of social and political idealism arise, according to the views of the psychoanalytic school, from the fact that psychic energies can be invested in socially approved objects, giving them a certain emphatic value. The great problem for the sociologist to-day is to find ways in which to use these energies in a socially valuable way.

We have seen that idealisation and sublimation, special forms of what we call, more generally, the displacement and transference of psychic energy, use the very same energy which is used with quite different results in the case of neurotic symptoms or rationalisations or reaction formations. Whether energies are to be invested in socially approved objects depends, of course, on the individual character, but perhaps even more on the nature of and the guiding forces at work in the society in which he lives.

We are living in a period in which the idea of social planning is not at all a strange conception. It is very probable that the guidance of our psychic energies will sooner or later be considered as an important social problem. Such guidance, of course, does not mean that we could or would want to regulate our individual development in a mechanical fashion or that we should try to forecast the evolution of a given individual. This is neither possible nor desirable; but it is fairly possible that the general factors which tend to mould human behaviour and shape the utilisation of superfluous psychic energies may be so collected and guided as to influence the majority of the population to a certain degree and in certain directions. One should distinguish here between two entirely different things: the first is the shaping of a certain individual in a pre-determined way, enlisting the help of certain institutions to produce a specific type of individual. If anyone believes in the possibility of shaping a person in this way, he must assume a considerable degree of predictability and inevitability in society. This is not at all our view. We assume a second position in which certain conditioned causations will produce some effects with a given statistical probability. But the freedom for growth beyond the type is an essential to this much more tentative and flexible kind of development.

The guidance of emotional energy in earlier societies consisted firstly of adjustments of the active energies according to needs of the society, such as those arising from the process of the division of labour, and secondly in adjusting the superfluous energies by stimulating the growth of sublimation patterns, by influencing leisure activities and so on. We must study very carefully how in older types of societies sublimation and transference of psychic energies and emotions were guided.

6. OBJECT FIXATION AND TRANSFERENCE OF THE LIBIDO

The possibility of the guidance of emotional energies is provided by the fundamental fact that human emotions are not at birth all fixed on certain objects and it is very often the social situation which links them up with definite objectives. If an emotion is once linked up with an object, we speak about object-fixation or *kathexis*. Such fixations are, for instance, the love of children for parents and parents for children, of sisters and brothers, of teachers and pupils, of playmates, but they can include also certain non-personal objects like the home, or activities like work and games, and finally religious or political symbols or beliefs. Once the fixation has taken place, the bond may become firmly secured, but there is, nevertheless, usually a possibility of shifting the libido from one object to another.

In the same way as there is an evolution in the child's life in respect of the general models of imitation from persons near at hand to those more remote and from concrete to abstract models, there is also a transference of emotions, originally fixed on the mother and other members of the family, to members of the community outside the family and finally even to the abstract idea of community itself. Further, just as the basic situation for every kind of human sociability is founded on the fact that the human child is more dependent than the young animal, so the fate of the libido is determined by the same basic situation. During the period of suckling and protection, the child develops feelings of dependence which lead to the development of the libidinous tendencies and these emotional tendencies are integrated and fixed upon one person, usually the mother. As the first fixations occur during earliest childhood, the early family pattern will be critically important for the individual, in helping to create his fundamental attitudes. Lasswell stresses the fact that the adult mind is only partly adult and consequently introjected objects and models of early childhood may influence adult behaviour in social situations. One can very often observe that grown-up children in their behaviour reflect the attitudes of their mother. Feelings of anxiety, superstition patterns and taboos might be at work which were taken over from a parent and be at work even in adult life. Every family, therefore, exhibits many of those patterns of behaviour and attitude which the mother and the father might have brought from their own families. This partly explains the slowness of the development of society even in dynamic or revolutionary periods. This slowness is not due to the fact that the individual cannot be transformed, but rather to the fact that the fundamental moulding unit, the family, works for a long time in the same way, even if the social surroundings have changed. It is not the biological and the mental inheritance which is the reason why certain mental patterns are reproduced from generation to generation, but the fact that changes in public life penetrate only very slowly into the inner life of the family.

The child, once it has been moulded by the family, can only very gradually transform these primary patterns of action and of attitudes. Nevertheless, there is a period in the development of the child when the transference of an important part of libido fixation can take place. This is the period of puberty or adolescence. This phase of biological growth coincides with new social contacts and new social demands. A conflict of roles may emerge and the general, if not complete, displacement of emotional fixations may take place. There is a problem of adolescence in our society: youthful aspiration for autonomy and parental insistence upon dependence clash with each other. It is interesting that primitive societies have planned and institutionalised this transition in the customs connected with initiation rites.

In a symposium devoted to sociological research in adolescence M. Mead, E. B. Reuter, and R. G. Foster deal with different aspects of this problem. According to Reuter, adolescence should not be defined in terms of physical maturation. If we analyse it as a social experience, adolescence begins when society no longer looks upon the person as a child, but expects him to take over some adult responsibilities. The age at which this occurs depends on social and not on biological factors. Religious groups confer adult responsibilities—confirmation for instance—on children of 12 to 14 years. The age of consent in sexual matters in England is 16, for the serving of alcoholic drink is 18, for majority it is 21. Modern society tends to establish a long period of transition between childhood and maturity, while the adolescent usually considers himself an adult and urges in one way or another that family and society should no longer treat him as a child.

Sociologically, adolescence is a stage of social development and a state of mind; it represents an intermediate period of detachment of the young person from family control. There is a marked dependence upon his age-group, before he achieves the individual independence in making decisions, which is characteristic of the fully adult status. Many persons who are physiologically adult never really outgrow the attitudes and sentiments which we call adolescent.

Much depends upon the kind of patterns of behaviour and attitude which are offered to the young in the critical phase of growth. If a society could determine what it was appropriate to do in planning the vital influences and could decisively affect the two fundamental phases of development, infancy and puberty, individual difference would still arise but a greater guidance of society would be possible. Of course, even after puberty we constantly change our attitudes—mobile types do this more often than static types—but the common foundation would be greater. I believe that we are on the threshold of a situation in our society in which more guidance will be necessary.

That there is, even in later stages of social development, a continuous transformation and displacement of the libido can be shown by the fact that a revolutionary society is to a great extent characterised by a loosening of the previous fixations of the libido. The great tension in such a society arises from the fact that there are quantities of libidinous energies present, without any fixation,

31

seeking for a new integration. In a conservative, traditionalistic society, emotional energy is fixed upon members of the family, on friends, on members and on membership of the traditional group into which one is born, on the ambitions which are cherished in such groups and, in some cases, urge the individual to attempt to rise in the given social scale. At the same time, the emotional value of religious ideas, of social customs and traditionally cultivated games is still very great.

But once there is a general shifting in the structure of society, many people lose their social and political ambitions, their religious ideals, their recreational habits and their emotional investments in personal ambitions. As a result there is an amount of displaced unattached psychic energy which can be utilised for new purposes.

The creation of a new religion only becomes possible in a situation in which a new generation has loosened its old emotional ties and when leading groups realise, perhaps not very explicitly, that they must create new common emotional fixations which can be linked up with loyalties toward the new social order. Libido fixation in revolutionary periods or in epochs of reformation is usually brought about by such a process.

The sociological significance of displacement and of transference must be regarded as very important, in just the same way as the displacement of private motives from family objects to public objects constitutes the normal form of development in the individual. Thus, feelings of admiration and loyalty felt by the child toward parents can be later transferred to figures of public authority and to the fatherland. On the other hand, repressed hatred of one or other parent may be turned later against kings, capitalists or other persons of authority. As Lasswell has pointed out, an adult who has the feeling that he cannot love his monarch any more, may feel that he can love 'mankind'. He cannot love God, but he can love the Nation. Or he may feel unable to love his country and makes instead out of his class or party an object of love and veneration.

The question arises here whether and how far psychology is useful in a political analysis. My view is that analysis of politics without psychology is quite inadequate. But on the other hand, psychology alone is insufficient because psychology has a very important limitation: it tends to cut out the social factors, such as the development of institutions and of the technical apparatus of society and it neglects economic pressures and the needs and influences arising from strategic and military factors to which a society is exposed.

7. THE SOCIOLOGY OF TYPES OF BEHAVIOUR:

i. ATTITUDES AND WISHES

So far we have spoken about the most elementary processes which integrate, dissolve, reintegrate, fix and shift the libidinous psychic energy.

These developments belong to general systematic sociology because every society, the most primitive as well as the most complicated, is based upon these mechanisms. Historical sociology, on the other hand, ought to deal with the more individualised forms of libido fixations and displacements, such as the character of family sentiments in a certain historical period or the concept of love in the period of chivalry, or the feeling of nationalism in a country like Germany in different social groups, or the history of libido displacement in the life of different groups.

Between these two levels of sociology—systematic general sociology and historical sociology—there is an intermediate level. Here we study certain general types of behaviour and types of attitudes which are sufficiently definite to characterise a whole mental type and which enable us to apply our general statement in more concrete historical settings.

An example of such an analysis is offered by W. I. Thomas, the American sociologist and social psychologist, who worked out a group of types and called them 'the four wishes'. Thomas recognised that if we have the task of describing a certain group of people and we wish to describe not only their activities and objective adjustments but also the changes of their inner life, their attitudes, wishes and feelings, then we need a classification into which most people can be fitted. This means either that they belong completely to one type—which occurs rarely—or it means that they represent a mixture of two or more of these types. Thomas recognises that human wishes have a great variety of forms, but he thinks that they can nevertheless be classified with some advantage into the following four types:

The desire for new experience.
The desire for security.
The desire for response.
The desire for recognition.

Thomas thinks, and I agree with him, that complex attitudes derive from very elementary tendencies, drives or so-called instincts. He tries to reduce the four types of wishes mentioned above to the most elementary attitude patterns which can already be found in the life of the infant and at a primitive level of social evolution. It is necessary here to recapitulate both his descriptions of the fundamental wishes and his attempt to reduce these to simpler urges.

The desire for new experience. All experiences which have something in common with pursuit, flight, capture, escape or death, are exciting experiences. Thomas speaks of experiences here which characterised the earlier life of mankind. There is a slow transformation from the original to the most complex and sublimated patterns.

34

Even to-day we can recognise such a thing as the 'hunting pattern' of interests. 'Adventure' is the first transposition of this pattern. Sensationalism in newspapers is another kind of transformation. Such individual activities and experiences as courtship have in them also an element of pursuit. There is a hunting pattern at work in every genuine scientific investigation and the same applies to the solution of puzzles or problems.

The desire for security. This desire is based mainly on fear which accompanies the possibility of physical injury or death and expresses itself in timidity and flight. The individual dominated by the desire for security is usually cautious and conservative, tends to regular habits, systematic work and to accumulate property. The social polarity between the rebel and the traditionalist corresponds to the first two types of wish.

The desire for response. This desire has evolved from the tendency to love, to seek and to give signs of appreciation. We see this tendency at work in the devotion of the mother to the child and in the response of the child. But we see it at work on another level also in the desire for responses between the sexes. An ardent courtship for instance is usually full of assurances and appeals for reassurance. Jealousy is an expression of fear that the response is directed towards another person. However, social success very often leads to a reduction of the wish for obtaining personal responses.

The desire for recognition. This wish is expressed in the struggle of personalities for positions of influence and prestige in their social group. We call this a desire for social status. An obvious example is found in the case of the politician or the captain of industry striving for success. A man or woman may provoke responses and gain recognition through a feigned illness; others may gain distinction by a display of feigned or genuine humility, self-sacrifice, saintliness and martyrdom. The same tendency may be socially useful in one case and

35

noxious in others. The motives connected with an appeal for recognition through self-centred interest and ostentation we call vanity; whereas creative activities connected with the same wish are called ambition.

Some individuals are temperamentally predisposed towards certain classes of the above-mentioned wishes but the expression of the wishes is profoundly influenced by the approval or disapproval expressed by the person's immediate circle and by the general public or social environment.

Further, we must allow for the shifting from one category to another and also for the possibility of finding new objects for the same category. Finally, different wishes may be combined in the same individual's personality. An emigrant to America may wish to see a new world, to make a fortune, to obtain a higher standard of living, or any other of a number of possible examples of the working of each or all of these four wishes.

Character may be considered as an expression of the organisation of these basic wishes, resulting from the interplay of temperament and experience. The wishes are the starting points of activity and pressure is brought to bear on human behaviour by influencing human wishes.

ii. INTERESTS

So far we have considered the importance of the unconscious and irrational elements in human life. Although social life is undoubtedly guided to a large extent by unconscious and emotional factors, it would be a great mistake to overlook the role played by rational interest.

We shall distinguish two notions of 'interest': first, interest in a broader sense (e.g., 'I am interested in people . . . in art . . . in philosophy.'). This is interest in a purely psychological sense. The second notion we shall call rational interest.

Interest in the first, broader sense is the counterpart of attitudes. According to MacIver attitudes are subjective states of mind, involving the tendency to act in a characteristic way, whenever a stimulus is presented. Such attitudes are envy, abhorrence, contempt, worship, trust or distrust. All attitudes, of course, imply objects towards which they are directed; but it is the state of mind, not the object, which is denoted by the term 'attitude'.

When, on the other hand, we turn our attention from the subject to the object, we shall speak of an object of interest. A politician, for example, is an object of interest to many people although the attitudes of these people toward him may be very different.

We can start by considering an object of interest from the point of view of its subjective element. Once my interest has focussed on the object, however, the objective relationship between the object and me becomes more and more important. In this broader sense we can speak about interest in cultural objects, like a philosophy. In this case interest means objects which enlist our attention.

From interest, in the sense that I am 'interested in' a thing, we must distinguish interest which has the special implication of *personal advantage*, which we sometimes call self-interest. As an instance of this I may want to get the greatest amount possible in the fields of power, prestige or economic gain. It is principally the wish for advantage which urges me to purposive activities. This means that interest compels me to organise my behaviour to attain this given end of calculation, and in this case we can speak about the second sense of interest mentioned earlier, *rational interest*. This implies calculation and striving for a given end and is a complex form of adjustment, because calculation implies choosing the means which lead most effectively to that end in the shortest way with the greatest economy of effort. 'It implies a positive control over the sources necessary to carry purposes into effect and possession of the means to satisfy desires and the trained powers of mind and particularly of initiative and

37

reflection required for free preference and for circumspect and farseeing desires.'

For instance, while the group based upon blood relationships (the family or the clan) prevails, the individual is so strongly bound to his family or his clan that he is unable to free himself from the common regulations and taboos. In this case he does not orientate his activities according to his personal interests, but according to the group interpretation of the situation, except that he realises his personal interests in those of the group. Tradition is decisive in such a situation, as Malinowski has shown us in his description of the economic life of the inhabitants of the Coral Islands, where prices do not follow the law of supply and demand, but follow tradition.

If I am striving for a certain good, which others also want to obtain, each for himself, we speak about *like interests*. If two or more persons pursue an aim, which remains a unit for them, which they think is a whole, we speak about a *common interest*. Whereas like interests lead to competition for the same good, common interests lead to co-operation. One of the most important problems for every harmonious society is how to turn like interests into common interests—how to turn competition into co-operation. This implies the guidance of libido-transference.

Another important distinction is that between *long run interest* and *short run interest*. If a man is in the habit of changing his wishes and interests, he will not be able to organise his behaviour in line with long term objectives. Examples for such behaviour are furnished by the spoilt child who always demands and receives fulfilment of immediate wishes, or the vagabond who has no definite aim in life.

One of the most important conditions for the growth of organised activities, and all self-organisation or life-organisation, is the creation of long run interests, and private property has been among the most significant forces in history creating a long run interest in the individual. Any complex system of production or social organisation needs long run activities and in the leading groups these activities were mostly created by private property. But they can also be created by organised common interest based on consciousness of common property, or by premiums given to the greatest common achievement. Examples can be found in the attitude of loyalty to a code or ideal found in Britain in, say, the soldier, the sportsman, the civil servant and also seen in the Soviets in successful cases of so-called 'socialist competition'. Compulsion gives poor results, and slaves are the poorest workers. Private property and efforts based on incentives of honour or advantage give better results.

Private property enforces long run calculation, which in turn reorganises the behaviour of the individual. The precise nature of the interest and of the organisation of behaviour varies according to the kind of property. Landed interest, for instance, creates a much greater libido fixation on the concrete object than money interest, which creates an abstract type of libido fixation on money *in abstracto*, that is, on the amount of money or the kind of goods. Landed interest, on the other hand, encourages a sense of belonging, of winning a living from the soil by personal striving and by 'understanding' the earth and the people who work it.

The creation of disinterested behaviour in society is a very important problem which will occupy us again and again. It is stimulated by the fact that there is a more or less long chain of intermediate links between the first and last steps of our activities. The man who belongs to a socialist party, for instance, has perhaps not ever the chance to see the aims of the movement to which he belongs attained during his lifetime. Thus, not only property, but every kind of co-operation and division of labour increases opportunities for abstract behaviour,

39

develops the capacity to prolong the tension between wishes and their fulfilment.

The social integration of wishes and attitudes differs very largely from the integration of interests. The integration of interests is mostly performed by compromise, which means, for instance, that people with like interests, who compete for an advantage, resign one part of their advantage on the basis of a rationalised agreement. All barter consists in such a renunciation of expected advantages and every kind of association is the result of an integration of interests.

The integration of attitudes, on the other hand, is performed on the basis of direct identification. This implies that we identify ourselves with the other members of a community and also with the community as such. Modern society, establishing long-run interests, tends to repress the libidinous element from the field of public activities and from work, and this may be a serious handicap in certain social activities and situations.

PART 2

THE MOST ELEMENTARY
SOCIAL PROCESSES

CHAPTER III

A. Social Contact and Social Distance

We are not concerned any longer with the psycho-logical equipment of the human individual, but with those elementary social processes which immediately affect his development. I shall only deal with a few of these, but they are of such fundamental importance that no individual and no social life can be fully understood without a certain knowledge of them. Such social processes are, for instance, social contact, social distance, and isolation.

Sociologists, who prefer to state only the phenomena of the so-called Great Society, such as social mobility, social stratification and social institutions, without linking up these studies with the observation of the minutiae of the elementary social processes are not likely to present an account which is as true as it might be.

1. PRIMARY AND SECONDARY CONTACTS

We must distinguish two kinds of contacts: the *primary* contacts, those developed in intimate, face to face associations, where visual and auditory sensations are always engaged; and *secondary* contacts, which are characterised by externality and greater distance. People who are mentally shaped by primary contacts, primary virtues and ideas, develop different characteristics from those who are shaped by secondary contacts. As an example compare the woman who is mainly a wife and a mother with the managing director of a factory or a

43

politician. There are, of course, connections between personality traits developed by primary and by secondary contacts. The wish for public recognition by the operation of psychological displacement is often, at least in part, a substitute for the lack of intimate responses within the family.

It is clear that the natural area of secondary contacts is the city. The Industrial Revolution by building cities and by breaking up small units of social life like the village, was the most important agency in creating a great number of abstract and impersonal relationships. The secondary contacts thus created operate in such a way that they promote the abstract attitude; they enable us to compare facts and to develop long-term interests and calculations, because 'trends' can be worked out and new systems of controlling people by emphasizing the different parts they play as taxpayers or workers, can be devised. The face to face situation, dominated by primary contacts, has thus been transformed.

2. SYMPATHETIC AND CATEGORIC CONTACTS

There is also another classification of contact which shows how the primary and secondary classifications come into being from a psychological and sociological point of view. People who do not belong to our group do not fall into the realm of our primary contacts. We do not consider them as real individuals, but we categorise about them. This means that we classify them in terms of different degrees of sympathy or antipathy. Here we find the social origin of prejudices. The feelings of sympathy connected with the different categories and groups create the so-called prejudices against persons whom we can classify, for instance, as Negroes, Germans, Jews, aliens, foreigners, 'them'.

The first phase of this process of categorisation is a

44

primitive kind of adjustment. We start by denoting or defining groups by convenient signs, because we are not able to deal with every object with which we come into contact, distinctly and separately. Further, if we meet an unknown fellow-being for the first time, we usually feel a sudden sympathy or antipathy. This is obviously an interpretation of the attitude, so common in animal life, where sympathy and antipathy are a kind of tool of selection for possible experiences. Our understanding is, further, in most cases determined by the notions and prejudices we have. The natural basis of prejudices is a propensity to fit new experiences into old categories by using early generalisations to cope with new experiences. Every real experience is based upon immediate contacts. Understanding is a battle between immediate readiness for new versions of experience and the propensity towards prejudice. People who are mobile, socially or geographically, are more critical and unbiased in judging others and less prejudiced, because they are used to getting into touch with various people. 'Rooted' people are, as we know, more inclined to prejudice. The mobile people may more easily move from categoric experiences into specific experiences.

The importance of the first impression you have in a great city stems from the fact that it reacts upon your self-consciousness and self-evaluation. The self-consciousness of the city dweller is unstable and flexible; whereas in the village, prestige is based on who your father is, to which family you belong and your position in the community, in the city prestige is based much more upon personal achievement. As a result, the city dweller is often more isolated and his self-evaluation is internalised.

A result of this is the flexibility, but also the instability, unsureness and scepticism in the character of the city dweller. Further, the relative anonymity of the individual in a great city increases the spheres of life within which we are able to turn over responsibility to somebody else.

As a result of this, more and more people get used to the situation of being spectators.

The categoric element in personal contacts disappears in real friendships. These are based on sympathetic contacts, which means a wish for identification of interests. The expression 'we' implies mutual identification and diffusion of personalities. Our 'neighbour' in some senses is essentially ourselves. The more individualised people are, the more difficult it is to attain identification. Instead, ambiguous feelings regularly arise within the medium of identification, and the feeling to be different is stronger. Friendship and marriage are relationships which channel more or less successfully this ambiguity.

The locus of earliest experience of social unity and identification are face to face groups such as families, self-governing play groups, neighbourhoods, clubs, fraternal societies or colleges. Sentiments of love, hero worship and courage but also of ambition, vanity and resentment are being shaped in these groups. According to Cooley, love, freedom and justice are primary ideas, they are at the root of Christianity, democracy and socialism, all three being based upon the ideas of primary groups.

Contacts within and without the group have been analysed by sociologists like Sumner, Cooley and Burgess. According to them internal sympathetic contacts and group egotism result in a double standard of feeling, thought and action : good-will, co-operation and trust between the members of the group, but hostility and suspicion toward the members of other groups. The relation of comradeship in the in-group and hostility towards others (the out-group) is correlative. The exigencies of struggle with outsiders strengthens the solidarity within the group so that internal discord should not weaken it.

Ethnocentrism is the technical term for this attitude. One's own group is everything and all others are rated in reference to it. Each ethnocentric group nourishes its own pride and vanity, its superiority, exalts its own divinities and looks with contempt on outsiders. This contempt is expressed by using terms of derogation to name and characterise other groups such as 'pig-eater', 'cow-eater', 'uncircumcised'. What underlies these judgments we may call gentile morality. Nationalism is obviously based on this attitude of prejudice and gentile morality.

3. SOCIAL DISTANCE

In every kind of social contact there is implied a social distance. Distance may signify an external or spatial distance, and an internal or mental distance. The whole variety and diversity of social and cultural life would be inexplicable without the category of social distance. Without it there would be objects and persons but not a social world. Distancing is, at the same time, one of the behaviour patterns which is essential to the persistence and continuity of an authoritarian civilisation. Democracy diminishes distances. Prestige (for instance that of an officer in the army) is thus largely a matter of 'distance'. Literally, distance means rendering something remote, transferring an object which is near to a position which is farther away from the point of reference. The word 'distance' originates from our direct experience of space. Its peculiarity is that spatial experience provides the pattern for mental experience too. That somebody is, for instance, at a distance of five feet from me is a spatial experience, but if I say that somebody is socially distant from me this means that I have either a higher or a lower social status than the other. There is a certain similarity between these two kinds of distances, although they are not identical. The sociologist speaks about creating artificial distance. What does he mean? Spatial distance, measurable in simple, physical terms, is being transmuted by a deliberate act of the human will into

47

something which may be called mental distance. To create mental distance implies diminishing identification. It is to move from sympathising acts towards alienation, without, however, necessarily implying categoric or aggressive behaviour.

First let me give an example in the field of purely sensory experience of how the fundamental process of distancing can be observed. A seafarer, on approaching the port may at first enjoy a clear view of the town that lies ahead. Suddenly the whole prospect is rendered remote because of a mist. Actually the town is no farther off than before, but the mist has artificially created the illusion of remoteness. In this example distance was not created by the subject, but by the mist. All mental distances with which we shall be concerned emanate from the spontaneity of the subjects; in fact, they are created by the subjects.

The evolution of mental distancing from spatial distance can be clearly demonstrated in the case of fear. In fact, the fear distance is the simplest distance. If I keep a safe space between myself and the stranger who is stronger than me, then, in this spatial distance between us there is contained the mental distance of fear. Caged animals, in a certain situation, preserve a spatial distance from one another in direct proportion to their relative strength.

Schjelderup Ebbe established on the basis of careful observation that there exists a well-determined hierarchy among social animals, for instance among hens, cocks and chicks. He observed them in groups of from two up to twenty-five and later in groups containing twenty-five to one hundred. According to him, the first thing that struck the observer was that during the search for food, during eating out of the food-pot or going to the perch to rest or going to the nests to lay eggs, the birds observed an exact order: the dominant bird always came first and the second, the third and all the other places were taken always by the same birds. The question arises how this order was shaped. Observation showed that it was shaped by fighting. When two chickens meet, the first thing is to establish, so to say, their social rank by fighting. The bird which runs away first, becomes for ever subjected. Thus, a complete list can be worked out according to the fighting results and it seems that this hierarchy is strictly observed by the birds. There is always a first one who dominates all the others and a last one who is dominated by all the others. The observation further established that the order of rank does not follow strictly the differences in bodily strength, but that what may be called psychological superiority, such as courage, also plays a great rôle. But it is an established fact that the fear distance is always at work.

The next task was to establish the typical behaviour of the leading birds and of the subjected ones. It seems to be a general rule that those at the top of the hierarchy are more benevolent than those who are in the middle of the social scale. It seems that when the rank of the leading bird is once established, it does not need to fight any more to maintain its position. The psychological fear distance has been established and is stable. But the birds in the middle of the hierarchy are very aggressive, as they are anxious to maintain their position, which is permanently threatened on two fronts.

The next task which the observers had set themselves was to find out how the same bird behaves in changing conditions. If you take a cock which is the leader of one group and put it in a group where it becomes one of the 'middle class' individuals, it changes its behaviour. Instead of being benevolent it becomes aggressive. Obviously it is anxious to keep its position. On the other hand, if you take a leading animal of a big group and make it the leading animal of a small group, it behaves more benevolently than it did as leader of the big group. This observation seems to make it very likely that behaviour depends more on social position than on inherent character.

The observers then tried to find the rule of social distance and social ranking among school children. They found that in a class of school children there is to be found a definite hierarchy, which does not coincide at all with the valuation of the school teacher, but is the outcome of the group life of the children.

If you take the leader of one group of children and put him into another group where he belongs to the 'middle class', his behaviour changes. Thus, amongst school children too, behaviour seems to depend on the social position of the individual as well as upon the so-called character, which seems to be to a great extent the result of varying social situations.

It is obvious that there are certain general tendencies inherent in group life as such, which work in the same direction, although they are altered by the mental equipment of the living beings composing the group. One of the main differences between animal behaviour and human behaviour in groups seems to consist in the fact that animals are incapable of organised action leading to revolutionary change. Only individual rebellion exists in animal groups. The subjected bird often improves its position by new fighting, mainly in cases in which the subjection was not due to bodily inferiority but to psychological fear which can be overcome. Observing such fights, one can see that the subjected animal is very excited, it attempts to overcome the traditional and established attitude of subjection, to overcome the fear distance. Révész, another student of animal sociology, observed the behaviour of caged monkeys. In the cage observed by him there were one leading animal, four weaker monkeys and one baby monkey. When food was brought to the cage there arose first an impulsive scramble, but this behaviour gave way very soon to a situation in which the strongest monkey was able to satisfy himself, without obstacle, as the first of the monkeys. The weaker monkeys driven by hunger made attempts to grab the food also, but suddenly seeming to remember the outcome of former fights and the beating to which they were subjected by the leading animal, they began to flee towards the opposite end of the cage. After this the baby monkey came forward and placing himself quite near to the leading animal started eating the bananas peacefully without being beaten by the tyrant. As long as the baby does not interfere with the competition of the other animals, he will be a privileged animal. But, the first time he participates in the competition he will be subjected to the same fate as the other competing animals. It seems that in every typical situation a certain distance again and again reproduces itself among the animals. The spatial distance contains here, at the same time, a distance of fear and respect; the objective space tends to be correlated to us with qualities of mental distancing.

The German expression *drei Schritt von Leib* (three steps from the body) used to characterise the attitude of keeping one's distance, expresses well a state of society in which spatial distance expresses at the same time fear and respect. One pace is the normal distance between members of a society. A distance of three paces is being imposed on persons outside the dominant 'group' as a mark of subordinate status in rigidly hierarchical societies. This is over-distancing and it can be opposed to under-distancing which is an expression of intimacy. Intimacy is correlated to a close, physical contact into which the individuals are brought—here again mere objective space tends to be correlated with qualities of mental distancing.

During the process of differentiation more complex types of distancing emerge from the fear distance; for instance, the power distance. The conventional distance which has grown up in a society strictly in response to the need for personal safety, has developed in many societies into a symbol of power relationships and into a fixed impression of the hierarchy of social rank.

We have to distinguish three kinds of distancing: distancing which guarantees the maintenance of a given social order and hierarchy; existential distancing, and self distancing, that is, creation of distance within a single personality.

4. MAINTAINING SOCIAL HIERARCHY

The hierarchical structure of a social order, the existence of social classes and estates is, in most cases, supported by a definite kind of distancing. The distancing apparent in social intercourse and in the selection of cultural objects belonging to that society, maintains a social stratification by mental means which tend to replace force. A very sophisticated system of dress and manners, speech, deportment and conventions can serve to keep up distance between the ruling groups and the subjected ones. The hidden task of this system is to create distance and thus to preserve the power of the ruling minority.

Distancing expresses itself by moulding social intercourse and by distancing certain objects in the cultural surroundings of a given society. Social intercourse can be moulded in two ways: first by limiting or excluding the co-operation between two groups (for instance, the prohibition of intermarriage, or of eating at one table), second by working out a sophisticated system of usages which accentuates distance between the different strata of society.

By a sudden integration of the subjected majority every ruling group could be overthrown. Therefore, the principle of divide and rule is usually followed by the ruling group and if successful it assures the stability of the system. But not only social intercourse within each social stratum and between the different social strata is guided by distancing; the objects of the social and cultural environment are distanced in the same way. If we look at different societies and ask ourselves what can be distanced, we find that both man (like the leader and the king) and objects (like relics) can be. In primitive societies, for instance, the divine character of the leader, of the chief or of the king is due largely to the elaborate ceremonial which surrounds him and separates him from his subjects. The figure of a saint, on the other hand, becomes a relic mainly by elevating it spatially and thus isolating it from the worshippers. Further, sentences, sayings and proverbs can be separated from common use by incantation, like sentences taken from a sacred text by a priest. One can isolate institutions and organisations or spheres of life and activity, like art or holidays.

There is a similarity between the distancing of social intercourse and the distancing of the objects of the cultural surroundings. The artificial heightening of certain values, and the distancing of certain everyday habits sustain the same system. The ideals of chivalry (such as heroism, courtesy, large-mindedness) elevate and isolate certain behaviour patterns and raise demands which cannot be satisfied by the average man. Thus they have the same social function as the distancing at work in social intercourse.

Democratic evolution is characterised by the tendency either to diminish distancing or to change the methods of distancing. Whilst in pre-democratic society strict rules determined the dresses which could be worn by different ranks, democratic society replaced the old system by 'fashion'. Deportment and intercourse became freer. A process of levelling up and levelling down developed and free self-expression replaced, to a great extent, the traditional regulated ceremonial.

The inhibition of free self-expression can also serve as a means of social distancing. Thus, the higher ranks can constrain themselves to preserve a certain kind of deportment or dignity.

5. EXISTENTIAL DISTANCING

This kind of distancing can be observed if we rule out all acts of distancing which have a social origin. That there exists a certain form of distancing other than the social kinds can be shown by the following example: if a woman of a humble social status visits a priest for the sake of confession, he is for her not a specific person but a personality representing an elevated social status. But, at the same time, she may be affected by her closeness to or remoteness from his purely personal self, the man as she experiences him. It is this last distance which we can call *existential distance*. But these two kinds of distance are usually confused. The social mask and the personal, existential character usually act simultaneously. The democratising process, as a rule, tends to diminish social distance and uncover the purely existential relationships between men.

Existential difference denotes a relationship between individuals which arises exclusively from the qualities of the inner spirit of man. It can be observed when somebody becomes suddenly aware of a sympathy with another human being and he establishes, so to say, an immediate contact with his innermost nature. This inevitable existential distance is that which remains after all social distancing has been forgotten. Existential distance was for a long time obscured in most societies by social distance, as for example in caste societies, and it is the rise of individualism which has torn the social mask finally from the person.

6. THE CREATING OF DISTANCE WITHIN A SINGLE PERSONALITY

An individual can be near or far from his own essential being, in the same way as he can be near or far from the essence of another person. We can observe within an individual the phenomenon of being far from one's self, suddenly gaining possession of one's self and being self-estranged. The democratic age has undermined the range of social distances but has thereby accentuated the existential distance to a greater extent. Self-estrangement, which in certain cultural climates is inescapable, restrains the self-expression of the individual. Sudden gaining possession of one's self is the experience of which religious mystics or inspired artists like Dostoievsky often give a moving description.

Distancing is a most important factor in the transmutation of the power structure into mental and cultural patterns. History shows that changes in the style of culture are closely linked with changes in the power structure. The sociology of culture has to deal with these problems in a more detailed way and has to find out how the various historical kinds of power organisation react upon the various forms of mental distance.

CHAPTER IV

B. Isolation

1. THE SOCIAL FUNCTIONS OF ISOLATION

Isolation is the marginal situation of social life. It is a situation deprived of social contacts. The simplest forms of isolation are created by barriers, like mountains, inland seas, oceans or deserts. Natural barriers create very often a protective kind of isolation. Both groups and individuals can be isolated and in both cases the most important consequences of isolation are individualisation and retardation.

Every individual and every group once excluded from connection with other individuals or other groups tends to develop into an individual or a community which deviates from the others. That is to say it goes its own way; it adjusts itself only to its peculiar conditions, without exchanging influences and impressions with other individuals or groups. In consequence of a lack of contacts with others, the individual or group does not know of the evolution of other persons or social units. A phenomenon which we call disproportionate evolution emerges in this way. Social contacts act rather like contacts between physical objects with a different degree of heat. The contact of materials equalises the respective heats of the objects and they all tend to get the same degree of heat. Something similar happens to social classes. Frequent contacts between the aristocracy and the middle classes tend to make them, in many respects, similar, or at least decreases the dissimilarity existing between them.

On the other hand, isolation and distancing increase their original differences and individualise them. You can see this happening in rural communities which are isolated by mountains or marshes, and also in individuals who withdraw from others and seclude themselves. They all become 'peculiar'.

One must recall at this point that isolation operates already within the process of zoological evolution, and contributes to the creation of the various species. Adaptation of species is intimately connected by specialised organic adaptation to varied geographic conditions. Something similar can be observed in group life and evolution. For instance, if a unified, wandering, nomadic group settles down on a given territory and the result of this settlement is that the various sub-groups separate from each other and remain without contact for a long time, both their habits and their speech will start to differentiate. That is how dialects arise, in a way which is very similar to the arising of species and variation in animal life. Thus, individualisation and specialisation are one of the possible consequences of isolation.

The other possible consequence is retardation. Obviously a certain amount of isolation is necessary to every kind of individualisation. The individual must sometimes withdraw from society, withdraw into himself, if his personality is to be preserved from dissolution and is to retain its wholeness, but if the individual completely separates himself from society, a retardation of his evolution can be expected.

Similarly, the establishment of a successful race or stock of animals requires an alternation of periods of inter-breeding (the so-called endogamy) in which periods the characters are fixed, and periods of outbreeding (exogamy) in which the fresh blood is being introduced.

Sects living for hundreds of years isolated among people of another culture are an example of the rule that isolation promotes the stability of types. On the other hand, the mixture of different stocks which takes place for instance in North America, shows that lack of a certain isolation creates a great variety and instability of types. As already mentioned the essence of social isolation is the diminution of contacts. In this section we have reduced the complex forms of isolation to elementary processes. Our next task is to discover what are the various causes which create isolation and to detect what consequences may arise from the various forms of isolation.

2. THE VARIOUS KINDS OF SOCIAL ISOLATION

We distinguish two main types of isolation: spatial isolation and organic isolation. *Spatial isolation* can be external, an enforced deprivation of contacts, as happens when somebody is banished from his community or imprisoned. As a result, the individual will be deprived of the protection of his group, or, in the case of an animal, his herd. It is very significant that the masculine leading animal, if detached from the herd, is known by hunters to be extremely dangerous. He becomes more easily aggressive and is then much more wild than animals which remain in contact with the herd. Somewhat similarly, the banished, the imprisoned and to some extent, also, the outsiders of society, show a greater propensity for anti-social behaviour. It is interesting that in German the word for 'miserable' and the word for living in a foreign country have a similar root. Anti-social behaviour, sometimes even thirst for vengeance, is the typical mental consequence of imprisonment in solitary confinement, which is an extreme form of enforced seclusion. Many well-meaning people, influenced exclusively by traditional, religious and moral views, hoped at the beginning of the nineteenth century, that solitary confinement and loneliness would improve the character of convicts and would facilitate their conversion. The consequences,

58

however, were in most cases melancholic mental states, sexual abnormalities, sometimes even hallucinations and usually anti-social behaviour. The explanation for this is simple: the adjustment to the conditions of imprisonment imply, for most individuals, to become unaccustomed to society and social life and just this creates anti-social attitudes.

By *organic isolation* we mean symptoms of isolation which are caused not by externally imposed privation of contacts but by certain organic defects of the individual, such as blindness or deafness. The essential consequences of such defects are the lack of certain experiences common to all healthy men. Beethoven expressed this forcefully when he said: 'My deafness forces me to live in exile.' The consequences of the organic defects are very similar to social defects such as shyness, mistrust, inferiority or superiority feelings and pedantry. These social distortions are either the consequence and symptom of previous isolation, or they themselves create partial isolation. The consequence of such lack of experiences are that the deaf, the blind and the shy seldom get complete answers from normal people, that they are handicapped in every kind of public communication, that they become suspicious, distrustful and irritable and thus they have also less chance to choose their friends and comrades among those who are suited to them. We can then speak of 'lack of associations by choice' and the further result of this is a narrowed range of people with whom one can develop intellectual potentialities. All this may lead to resignation: the individual may give up the hope of obtaining a normal position and place in life or might even become a broken personality who accepts his role of imagined inferiority. Another frequent outcome of such a situation is compensation or even overcompensation for the disability, and a superiority complex might thus develop. Such a person might feel that 'nobody is good enough for me'.

Closely connected with these complexes is pedantry. The pedant is usually a person who only feels himself safe if he is under secure, reliable guidance, for instance under the harmonious shelter of home-like circumstances. Orderliness and cleanliness may mean for such people a protection against unforeseen frictions, collisions and criticism. Pedantry is mostly a symptom behind which there is a fear of coming into unexpected situations. So the pedant tries to define each situation in his own way. His precision has often been considered as a distorted form of scholarship. What distinguishes the pedant is the psychological compulsion, the inflexibility of mind and sympathy of which the exactitude is a fetish symptom.

Shyness is, in sociological terms, a kind of partial isolation which arises from an inability to make adequate responses in certain spheres of life. It is mostly a consequence of psychic shock suffered during childhood. This shock often occurs at the very moment when the child leaves the sphere of family and neighbourhood relationships and penetrates into the realm of secondary contacts. A kind of trauma, a psychic lesion, is the consequence of such a step, and chronic disturbance of the personality is observable. However, the seeds of shyness are to be sought in the familiar relationships during the first few years of life.

Shyness, arising at first only occasionally, tends to be later habitualised and can create all the symptoms of partial isolation. Early stages of such disturbances of the social abilities can be discovered in very young children, and later can appear as a general anxiety about meeting new situations. Such feelings arise, for instance, before examinations or even in the classroom when the child is afraid that he will be unable to answer unexpected questions. If this attitude becomes transferred to a later stage of development, it can hinder the normal decisiveness of the individual. An unbalanced personality very often attempts to compensate himself in some way or another,

60

if the usual family support disappears, by outbursts of feelings, the seeking of tenderness, sudden strong attachments to other people, and by other similar intense expressions of emotion.

Another kind of partial isolation arises when a normal ability to make social contacts cannot find a suitable surrounding needed to elicit responses. As an example we can quote the situation of the spinster and the bachelor—celibacy is sometimes the consequence of shyness. Personalities in such situations will seek for some satisfaction for the losses which they may experience in their personal and social lives, by finding a career of social usefulness, by friendship, if they can face it, by spiritual discipline, or perhaps by keeping pets and preserving a general sentimentalism.

3. FORMS OF PRIVACY

Privacy itself also represents a certain type of partial isolation. Privacy implies that the sphere of our inner experience is protected from being affected by social contact. Modern man often attempts to withdraw part of his inner self from public control. Here we can speak of the privacy of our inner self.

We can see a similar development on the social and political plane when we observe how the modern liberal state refrains from interfering with the privacy of the individual, in so far as it abstains from regulating or controlling private conscience, private convictions and private feelings, or when, in the modern city, we see a protection of the private life of the citizens from the public view. The life of the village does not know either internal or external privacy. In a village, or a primitive community, personal intimacy and public life are not so strongly opposed to one another as in the modern city. With the home life and problems of a peasant usually the whole village is concerned. Public control penetrates into every hidden nook of the life of the families of the individual. Why is this so? Obviously because in primitive communities the range of activities of the single individual is connected with the scope of activities of the whole community. Social separation, the withdrawal of one's personality, is, in such groups, extremely difficult. The guild of the medieval cities was equally able to control most of the external and internal activities of its individual members, such as the expressions of religious belief, their professional activities, the forms of sociability, their artistic activities, their funeral ceremonies. Modern organisations, like professional associations or corporations, touch only certain limited spheres of the individual. The possibility of escape into privacy is here much greater and by escaping, modern man successfully isolates one part of his inner self. This isolation means a strengthening of individualisation.

The religious movements, Protestantism and Puritanism, represent a tendency to transform public religion into private religion and to keep certain parts of the inner self safe from external interference. Puritanism also reflects the tendency to deprecate publicity and to increase the estimation of our private inner experiences. This process of creating privacy starts—like most of the inner transformations—with external changes, such as the separation of the home from the workshop or of the home from the office. The burghers of the later Middle Ages and of the Renaissance, becoming richer, could provide for every member of the family a room for his own use. These are the main external circumstances which create a set of attitudes and feelings which we call private. This is one of the forms of individualisation.

We must, here, clearly distinguish between attitudes connected with primary contacts, sympathetic contacts (such as intimacy) and attitudes connected with privacy. Privacy is a kind of isolation within the realm of the family or within other primary groups. It is a way of escape in a social group where the group control is very near to the individual. Privacy is an important aid in the creation of individualisation; it nurtures the tendency to internal individualisation. One of the main consequences of privacy is the creation of a double standard of norms, both of legal norms and of the moral norms of the conscience. But another consequence is the emergence of a double standard in the experience of time. Speaking of time here we do not mean chronological time, which can be measured with the help of an objective scale, but the way we are *aware* of time in our inner experience.

Our inner experience of time is mostly orientated on collective experiences. As long as we are intimately and firmly connected with our fellow beings through common aims, the tension invested in these common strivings differentiates time in a collective way for every participant. People acting together in order to bring about the same collective result measure the time according to their common activities. The articulation of events, even of time, was orientated originally on these common purposes. But privacy separates certain experiences of the individual from the community and the inner experiences become separated from the outer world. As a consequence, inner time is separated from the time of the community. It must also be remembered that disproportionate evolution creates individualised and inward experiences. Because these are private and personal, they are not equalised or levelled. The careful discrimination of experiences, connected with introversion is the source of subjective poetry and of subjectivism generally.

The danger of an excessive privacy is that it may lead to a split in the personality. The inner world of privacy and the world of common activities lose their inner connection and the person then lives in two separate worlds. Kretschmer and Sheldon have this schizoid response as characteristic of one of their psychological 'types'.

Privacy has, of course, also a productive significance for

culture if it represents not an absolute but only a partial isolation. This valuable aspect of privacy was observed by the organisers of the religious monastic movement. The cell of the monk is a means of artificially creating external conditions which favour privacy. Those who live in such cells are 'cloistered'. The regulations of the monastic orders contain the advice to avoid external contacts. The cell and these regulations helped to create artificially homogeneous fields of experience. The same aim is being furthered by the monastic regulations relating to work and leisure. It is here that we must look for one of the origins of subjective religious feeling. Such feeling is one of the early forms of inner individualisation fostered by privacy.

CHAPTER V

C. Individualisation

Privacy is only one of the forms of individualisation. There is a great variety of social forces which operate in such a way that they foster individualisation, and there are according to these various and diverging external forces, many forms of individualisation, by which I mean those social processes which tend to make the individual more or less independent of his group and to create in him a self-consciousness of his own.

In analysing how the processes of individualisation work two misconceptions must be corrected. The first is that individualisation is a process carried through solely by the individual himself. This is based on the assumption that a man frees himself completely or less completely from the influence of his group by the exercise of mental qualities alone. The second misconception is based on the assumption that individualisation is primarily a mental or spiritual process which is being spread through the prevailing ideas of a time or place. If historians, for instance, deal with the Renaissance, they collect sentences which prove that a new estimation of individuality has arisen at a certain time and within certain circles, and then show that these ideas were successively accepted later by other groups and other individuals. The task of the sociologist is not merely to observe that such ideas exist at certain times but to investigate *how* these ideas came to exist. We ask ourselves what the social forces were which engendered them in a smaller circle and which set of social influences prepared a larger group of people to accept them.

Ideas do not by themselves create individualisation. They are usually merely the mental expressions of the process of individualisation for which ground was prepared by social changes which were tending in this direction. Within the medium of such a new social texture expressed ideas do strengthen and decisively mould the new situation, but they do not create it. When I say that in every social situation there is a set of social forces with an individualising tendency at work, I am aware that certain periods such as the Renaissance or the period of eighteenth-century rationalism and nineteenth-century liberalism favour individualisation to a much greater extent than others.

In order not to confuse the various kinds of individualisation, I shall start by distinguishing their different forms and shall try to discover those particular social forces which favour each of these forms of individualisation.

I distinguish four main aspects of individualisation. Each of them can be further sub-divided.

The four main aspects are:

1. individualisation as a process of becoming different from other people.

2. individualisation on the level of new forms of self-regarding attitudes: either by becoming aware of one's unique and specific character, or by a new kind of self-evaluation or organisation of the self.

3. individualised relationships through objects: individualisation of the wishes.

4. individualisation as a kind of deepening into ourselves, that is a kind of introversion, which implies receiving into our experience of ourselves and sublimating the individualising forces around and within us. This can also be described as the disclosure of an inner dimension in man's life.

The four main aspects are therefore: becoming different; the rise of a new kind of valuation of our specific

66

character; individualisation through objects; and the introduction of the individualising forces. These four processes are entirely different phenomena.

1. INDIVIDUALISATION AS A PROCESS OF BECOMING DIFFERENT

The external differentiation of types and individuals leads to the formation of new groups in which these new characteristics can be commonly expressed. The emergence of such groups is accelerated by the division of labour and by the division of functions, the latter leading to the development of professional characteristics. Such new groups permit more or less individuality in their members, according to the intensity and volume of internal organisation and regulation. Compare, for example, the difference between the labour of the craftsman and of the operative in the factory. In the former the artisan works with his own tools, and the labour is more individualised. In the factory there tends to be an impersonal régime of labour rules. A further social factor conducing to the external differentiation of types and of individuals results from lack of contacts, when people thus isolated have eventually to adapt to varied conditions.

In old Chinese society, regulated by Confucianism, the conduct of man in all his relations was fixed. In domestic life, for instance, the rules of behaviour of the son towards the father or of the wife towards the husband or of the younger brother towards the elder brother were fixed. This of course influences both the opportunities open to the members of the group and their reality sense. On the other hand, democratisation in the broadest sense, political, economic and pedagogic, works powerfully in the direction of making spontaneous and untraditional action necessary. Free competition also compels the individual to adapt himself to his own peculiar situation, to seize the initiative and not to wait for commands or refer to rules. It is especially the small social unit, if it is organised in a democratic way, which favours the growth of personality. Such small social units were the canton states of central Switzerland, the free medieval commune, the sect. Similarly, democratically organised educational groups like the medieval universities facilitated individual efforts and decisions.

An obvious example of the facing of an unpatterned situation can be seen in the case of pioneers or merchant adventurers, who leave their original group with the aim of conquering new territory or creating new markets, or even when a young man or woman leaves the protection of the family to earn a livelihood in a new place. But competition within the group compels each person to act according to his individual interest and to re-interpret his own situation.

The process of individualisation is further fostered by the increase of social mobility, especially of vertical mobility which enables a person to rise in the social scale as an individual and not only as a member of his group. In this situation it is necessary for his success to free himself from group prejudice, though maybe later he adopts the prejudice of another group. Horizontal mobility, to be seen for instance in the wandering individual, implies the need for him to give up the old small group viewpoint. However, in this case, it may be impossible for him to identify himself wholly with the new group and in this way he is forced to find his own independent view. If you join an opposition group, you lose your original viewpoint and seek to learn and adopt another.

The situation of being an outsider, whether relative or absolute, has a similar individualising effect. Examples of a relative outsider are the neglected son of a family or the leader of an oppositional minority within a group, whereas absolute outsiders are outcasts, unassimilated aliens, banished exiles. The early life of Hitler, Lenin, Trotsky or Stalin shows many outsider situations.

The last social situation to be mentioned in connection with individualisation as a process of becoming different, is the escape from the social control of one group to that of another. In each group there is something different contributed and learned by the same person in company with different people forming different kinds of group—a family, a play group, a club, a university class. Thus a widened circle of contact can offer a more varied experience on which individualisation may develop with greater flexibility.

2. INDIVIDUALISATION ON THE LEVEL OF SELF-REGARDING ATTITUDES

From one point of view an individualised personality consists in becoming aware of our specific character and in the rise of a new kind of self-evaluation. Thus, the organisation of the self proceeds as forms of self-evaluation arise. Striking examples of this process can be found in history where the worship of the mighty personality creates a certain type of individualisation. The pre-conditions of this process are: a strict differentiation and distance of the leading *élites*; the organisation of the group in such a way as to provide for certain circles a chance to become despotic; the existence of the isolated milieu of a court where the despot can have the illusion of being powerful if not almighty. These are the preconditions for the making of a tyrant, resting upon physical power and spiritual coercion (often based on an attitude to his putative magical qualities) together with power deriving from land, property or money, and finally from prestige and glory.

A similar process can be observed in a more moderate form and in a narrow circle if a child becomes the tyrant of a family. We see in both cases the domination of

69

narcissistic impulses in the person of the despot, and this is accepted by his group.

A feeling of the uniqueness of one's life and character can be found at the origin of the cult of the autobiography. Its growth in the latest period of the Roman Empire is intimately connected with the emergence of the feeling that one's life and character are unique. But the origin of this feeling might be investigated even earlier in the death records of oriental despots. In this early stage of individualism, self-evaluation is founded on letting other people feed one's own sense of power by showing fear and respect. Examples of such self-glorification can be found in the annals of Assurbanipal (885–860 B.C.): 'I am the King. I am the Lord. I am the Sublime. I am the Great, the Strong; I am the Famous; I am the Prince, the Noble, the War Lord. I am a Lion. . . . I am God's own appointed. I am the unconquerable weapon, which lays the land of the enemies in ruins. I captured them alive and stuck them on poles; I coloured the mountain like wool with their blood. From many of them I tore off the skin and covered the walls with it. I built a pillar of still living bodies and another pillar of heads. And in the middle I hang their heads on vines. . . . I prepared a colossal picture of my royal personage, and inscribed my might and sublimity on it. . . . My face radiates on the ruins. In the service of my fury I find my satisfaction.'

Passing to the latest period of the Roman Empire and to the autobiography of stoic philosophers and statesmen we can point to the social situation favouring the strength of the feeling of uniqueness. We can point to the weakness of the organisation of the great society, and to the disrupted state of the empire, and connected with these the possibility for individuals to rise within the social scale. The weakness of the great organisation was such that its norms vanished away. We see here the dissolution of the ideals of the *polis*.

3. THE INDIVIDUALISATION OF THE WISHES THROUGH OBJECTS

In establishing the direction and constancy of feeling toward people and objects (what psychoanalysts call libido fixations or *kathexes*) the traditional attitudes and the durability of the primary groups are decisive. The peasant and the landed aristocrat are much more settled in their wishes than the rich mobile type of the city. The first seeks for a definite kind of wish fulfilment, whereas the second type has a standard in his attitude in so far as he wants to buy one thing or a certain kind of goods, but likes to vary the probabilities within these limits. His range of choice is likely to be wider and his actual choices more varied. Many factors increase the wish for sudden and individual choice—such as wealth, which creates the possibility of variations, or the process of modern production and distribution which favours individual competition and the man who is first in the field with a new idea; however, large scale industry which stimulates buying, also attempts to standardise consumer's choice. Besides these, there is social mobility, both horizontal (for instance, migration) and vertical (movements up and down the social scale), which tends to loosen the ties which bind the individual to specific wishes.

We might consider at this point some of the forms of the wish to possess. We can distinguish two: first, the attitude of possession toward single objects with definite libido fixation: second, libido fixation on abstract objects—for example, money, equality. Further, there are two kinds of wish attitudes to consider in connection with possessiveness—striving for a fixed object and striving for variety. In this latter case the libido fixed upon an object is, in a measure, shifted from the object to the choice itself. As examples of libido being fixed upon specific objects, we can quote the attachment of a peasant to his favourite pipe or to his favourite dishes at meal times, or to the landscape in which he moves. In all these cases the peasant is personally linked to his own property or to his personal situation. In the second case, where libido is fixed not so much upon objects but more upon the choice itself, we can quote the attitudes of those who follow fashion, of the liberal, or of the individualist in the competitive society. But even liberals and anarchists can have wishes for some anchorage in specific objects or people.

The strictly individualised libido fixation is shaped by the small family. For instance, libido fixation toward the mother and the father figures is greater in certain types of family than in others. In the primitive group-family, every child has several mothers and fathers, as in such families all mothers of the same age group are called mother by the child. In small monogamous families, the fixation is stronger and there is a deeply furrowed love of a mother observable in families with one child which is conspicuous if one compares it with families in which there are say ten children.

One of the main sources of individualised libido influencing notions of both unique personal and more general idealised love can be found here. Romantic love can only be explained in connection with introversion.

4. INDIVIDUALISATION AS A KIND OF INTROVERSION

By individualisation we understand a deepening of the personality; what could be called introjection. Its stages may be traced. The stage of estrangement, of becoming solitary, is characterised by the fact that the individual withdraws into himself his libidinous energy. We find this often in big cities where unfriendliness is felt and confusion is caused, and generally when the community loses its expressive force, when for instance forms of worship and ceremonies lose their collective and individual significance. The loss of the range of activities, the limitations of the possibilities of shared emotional expression, all contribute to estrangement, introjection and inwardness and to an introversion of the sublimating energies. This process combined with the emergence of individualised love makes romantic love possible.

There develops then an acceptance of privacy, partial isolation, as a means of escaping external control, as another form of individualisation connected with introversion. The predominance of introspection is also one of these forms. In the circumstances of social and cultural mobility when sudden inner readjustments become necessary, such introspective moods usually appear especially in personalities who have leisure time combined with privacy. Harmonious cultivation of the whole personality is the form of individualisation favoured by such people, who deal with things not specifically but as showing the variety and unity of experience at once. For such people, the social distance from the sphere of labour and social struggle results in a reduction of subservience to the power or finality of external facts. The great artists of the Renaissance, the writers and scientists of the seventeenth and eighteenth centuries, and some English thinkers of the nineteenth century, show these attitudes.

D. Individualisation and Socialisation

Where self-consciousness is dominant there is always a possibility of a predominance either of ourselves or of the self of the other person. If we say a person is selfish or self-centred, we think of him as being less able to see things and relations from someone else's viewpoint. Such a person has not wholly come through the first phase of social consciousness in which we see things only in their relationships to us. For example, children without brothers or sisters become very often especially self-centred. They are not socialised enough. By socialisation we understand a process which is the opposite of individualisation: it is a process of the expansion of the self. The expanding self follows certain lines which may be called the social access to the expansion of the self.

Sociologists have designated these various forms of expansion by symbolic terms such as the following:

The spheric self, which incorporates persons chiefly according to their propinquity. Persons in whom this aspect of self commonly appears care most for those they see most often, for instance their neighbours, and care little for those who are below their visual horizon. But reading, travel, city life and social stratification may stretch the radius of personality activities and thus are unfavourable for the development of this spheric self.

The linear self keeps to the family line, ranging back among ancestors and forward among anticipated descendants. It prompts a man to sacrifice much in order not to dishonour his forefathers or handicap his posterity. Family feeling is here a rival to wider social feeling.

The flat self emerges if social feelings are confined to the members of one's own social stratum. This horizontal socialisation weakens the barriers of jealousy which exist between neighbourhoods, parishes and provinces, but on the other hand creates new ones. Whilst hostile communities can avoid trouble by having little to do with one another, hostile social classes cannot avoid contacts and thus eliminate frictions in such a simple way.

The vein self. In big democratic cities, friendships and fellowships have a tendency to follow occupational lines. For instance, newspaper men identify themselves with and meet mostly other newspaper men. The fact that they are competitors is overshadowed by the community of interests they all possess. Those who do not love their

74

own calling and profession overmuch may follow a non-professional line of private interest.

The star self. The expanding self will, in some cases, get into sympathy with various sorts of people following up several veins. Thus arises the star self which radiates into various planes. As examples, we can point to the personalities of Goethe, Albert Schweitzer and Bertrand Russell.

The functional differentiation and complexity of modern society favour the development of the star self. The great number of matters calling for team work put a premium on the spheric self.

It is a future task of sociologists and teachers to find out which social situations foster the expansion of the self according to these and various other social axes.

However, it is important to stress that these terms must not be hypostatised into separable 'selves'. They have a limited practical usefulness for the sociologist. The profound question exists behind all such analysis, what is the nature of the self to which the processes of individualisation and socialisation have contributed?

CHAPTER VI

E. Competition and Monopoly

One of the most important social forces is competition. We can classify social forces into two groups: those which foster co-operation and those which compel people to act against one another, opposing each other. The main social force aiding people to act against one another is struggle. Struggle can be defined as a social relationship in which we wish to compel another person or a group by force to act according to our will. Hereby the resistance of the latter is to be overcome. Competition on the other hand can be considered as a kind of peaceful struggle and can be defined as a peaceful striving of several individuals or groups for the same good.

Competition, like struggle, is a universal category of life—in biology we speak about a struggle for life—and it is a general category of social life. Many people believe that competition is a purely economic phenomenon mainly represented by barter. But nothing could be more wrong than this limitation of the meaning of the word. The principle of competition is equally at work when any kind of race takes place, the common end being for each of several competitors to try to reach the goal first. But there is also competition when two different scientific schools attempt to solve the same problem, or if two men wish to marry the same woman. It is important to see that these different things all belong together because competition is at work in all these fields. Economic competition belongs to the same field—and in this connection it again becomes clear that economics is bound up with sociology.

Looking into the history of the idea of competition, it is interesting to note that the principle of competition was first observed in economics and was later transferred to the sphere of biology. Adam Smith and the Physiocrats were the first to work out a systematic account of competition. For them freedom and competition were necessary elements in the harmony of interests. Malthus, in his *Essay on the Principle of Population*, published in 1798, stated the discouraging view that there is a general tendency for the human population to increase in geometrical progression and for the fruits of nature to grow only in an arithmetical progress. It was Charles Darwin who in 1859 transferred the idea of competition to the biological sphere. He considered the life of living beings as a struggle for existence and came to the conclusion that this struggle urges the individual living organism to adjust himself to his peculiar situation. Thus Darwin, who was impressed by Malthus's *Essay*, developed the principle of natural selection by struggle for life.

It must not be forgotten that the essay of Malthus in its turn was a pessimistic reaction against certain optimistic social theories propounded by Godwin and Condorcet, who believed in the endless perfectibility and natural equality of mankind.

1. THE FUNCTION OF COMPETITION

We distinguish between personal competition and group competition. Although competition is prompted by personal aims, it discharges the social function of selection, especially of assigning to each a place in the social system. The chief alternatives to competition as a means of assigning to each individual his place in the system are the following:

(*a*) The assignment of social status through inheritance. (*b*) The principle of seniority. (*c*) The measurement of ability by forms of graded tests. A planned

77

society and all others which want to minimise competition might choose between these alternatives.

The amount of activity associated with the selection process in any society is an index of the intensity of competition. In a stationary society where, as a rule, children follow the occupation of their fathers, where certain positions are reserved for a limited number of castes; where the system of choice through a process of elections is unknown, a man expends a minimum of energy in finding a place in the social system. The intensity of competition varies with the degree of personal liberty, with the rate of social change and inversely with the nature of the selective agents.

The freer the individual in his choice of better paid or more highly esteemed occupations, the less often one encounters racial, religious or class discriminations, the higher will be the general level of achievement reached by a society.

Social change opens new opportunities to many who in other circumstances would believe themselves to be permanently and definitely settled. An impressive example of this process is the effect of the rising of the automobile industry in the U.S.A., which has in twenty-five years absorbed a million men, very few of whom might have inherited their jobs. The better the selective agencies are, the more economically and accurately are the competitors sifted.

2. SOME CONSEQUENCES OF COMPETITION

Every competitor tries to adjust himself as well as possible to his own peculiar conditions, in order to make the best of them and individualisation is a product of this adjustment in which the personal mentality of an individual reflects the structure of the situation and the peculiarities of the competitors whom he has to meet.

78

Competition heightens the versatility, the plasticity and the mobility of the individuals who take part in it. It is, in most cases, connected with social mobility. Only if I can move towards the best possible result is competition able to evolve its social potentialities. However, individual competition is an agency which tends to disintegrate group solidarity.

The place where competition originally arose was the market, which originated at the frontier of the tribe, that is, at the place where inter-tribal communication took place. The outlook engendered in this marginal situation penetrated later into the centre of society and the transformation into acquisitive society thus began.

Psychological competition tends to create inferiority feelings. This is a consequence of the means by which competition operates. I distinguish two kinds of inferiority feelings: those which make the individual active, urging him to adapt himself better to his situation (these feelings create new incentives and lead to reorganisation of the human personality); the second kind of inferiority feelings are those which paralyse the forces of the individual and compel him to accept his inferiority. The first kind of inferiority feelings are potential as well as actual, and in most cases are caused by a really free competition, whereas the second group of feelings are mainly fostered by the authoritarian behaviour of those who dominate an individual who is in a weak position.

The questions which emerge here are: Who is your competitor? How do you compensate for your inferiority feelings? Does competition increase your energies or are you meeting such situations by withdrawing yourself? Does competition encourage or discourage you in your efforts?

A minimum of inferiority feeling is often necessary for the discovery of new adjustments needed in new situations. It is the inferiority feeling which creates in the individual an urge to compensate for his inferiority. This

79

mechanism turns a bad performance into a good one in school, in the workshop and so on. But an excessive amount of inferiority feelings paralyses the activity of the individual as it disturbs the balance of his personality and his self-estimation.

There are, of course, also discreditable methods of dealing with one's manageable inferiority feelings. For instance, if, instead of developing our own faculties, we try to handicap our competitors, as when a mediocre leader in a bureaucracy chooses his assistants from among the ungifted and so makes possible the rule of the inferior. Or, again, to denigrate the ideas or personalities of competitors. In this way resentment against heroism or achievement may arise and a less effective group might attempt to incite others against those who are more efficient and successful, as, for instance, when a landed aristocracy seeks to create hostile feelings against industrial 'money-making'. A third and not uncommon way of dealing with our inferiority feelings is to seek for a scapegoat.

3. RESTRICTIONS OF THE METHODS OF COMPETITION

As long as competition works in a constructive way it will urge the individual to increase his personal efforts and incite him to bring about the greatest possible achievement. When competition works most effectively the result can be the selection of the best, both as to the dominant human type and the best performance in work. But there is a possibility that the same principle of free competition can produce just the opposite results and become a tool of a negative selection. Free competition must, therefore, always be accompanied by certain binding rules and accepted standards. The phenomenon of fair play here enters into the plan.

Fair play means that either in a whole society or at

least in one of its strata a certain social control prevails in the form of a standard of behaviour which governs the mentality of the competing individuals. Fair-mindedness can be introduced into competition at school, at games, in business life and in the political struggle. The group accepts, or is at least admonished by some of its members and leaders to accept, a governing social standard, which assures fair play among the competitors. Cooley was one of the first who realised the great social significance of this principle.

Among business competitors it is generally regarded that factory espionage is unfair. Some business men often successfully urge that the practice of local price cutting should be avoided. In the professions, like those of medical practitioners or barristers, it is regarded as unfair to advertise. In the case of elections the buying of votes or the threatening of the voters with reprisals by powerful individuals would be a violation of the principles of fair play. In advanced society nepotism in the case of a public appointment is considered unfair.

The principle of fair play had, of course, an important part in the development of English society and also in the development of the dominant English personality, particularly that complex stereotype 'the English gentleman'.

It would be worthwhile to investigate which social factors bring about and sustain the rule of fair play, and which social forces counteract it. It is probable that both the inner conditions of the competition itself and the general social background in which competition takes place influence the effectiveness of the binding rules. As to the inner conditions of the competition itself, it is quite obvious that a great increase in the number of competitors may be one of the causes of a lowering of standards among the competitors and may induce them to use unfair methods more and more often. The general moral standard of the whole society or of a closed group in it might, on the other hand, act as an agency which puts a brake on the process of competition. Sometimes it may be useful to institutionalise this social control, that is, to set up institutions which might be independent of the competitors and are empowered to control their behaviour. Such institutions might be courts, administrative boards, professional councils, arbitration committees and so on.

The remarks of Davis and Barnes on this subject illustrate the dangers of socially uncontrolled competition. 'Perhaps the greatest objection to the profit motive is that it destroys higher values. There is a sort of Gresham's Law for motivation and for social standards. The worst competitor may drag down the good to his own level or force him to bankruptcy. For example, if southern mills use child labour, northern mills claim they cannot do without it. The bad standards drive out the good, as paper currency drives out gold. . . . . We will have to face the necessity of revolutionising the incentives of our business life away from profits and towards the service of all.'

4. SOCIAL MONOPOLY

One of the typical processes which follows in the wake of evolution of free competition is its turning into its opposite: the emergence of a closed group, possessing monopoly. In order to understand the significance of this very important social phenomenon we must introduce a distinction between the *open group* and the *closed group*. We say that a social relationship or a social group is an *open* one, when nobody is excluded from participation in its activities. We call it a *closed* one when the participation in these activities is bound to certain regulations and when not everybody is allowed to share in these activities. There are groups which are interested in seeing that as many people as possible should join their activities (for instance, political parties). On the other hand, it is more advantageous sometimes to the participants of a group that their membership should be limited. The guilds, at the time of their early beginnings, were interested in being an open group because an increase in their number increased their fighting capacities. Later, when the number of handicraft men seemed to increase to a dangerous degree and the supply of goods rose, they began to be interested in closing their doors to these newcomers.

A *monopoly* means the limiting of the chances of success prevailing in a given social scope of action to a certain limited number of people. The consequences of the closing of a group are immense, as far as the mentality of its members is concerned. People belonging to a closed group behave quite differently from people who are members of an open group. The members of a closed group tend to become narrow-minded, and may become intolerant and hostile to anything which does not fit into the framework of their prejudices. Another typical consequence of the closing of the group is the development of a strongly held *esprit de corps*. The reason for this prevalence of a narrow frame of mind is due mainly to the fact that the lack of fluctuation permits the mentality of a certain type to prevail. Both the individuals and their group tend to lose their faculty of adjustment and a strong traditionalism develops. However, there are cases when the closing of a group may have some advantage. For instance, when a sudden influx of elements of a lower standard threatens the morals and the acquired qualities of a group. The closing of the group may help to preserve these qualities.

The closed group can establish different types of inner organisation. It may either permit or rule out competition within the group. In the first case, a certain improvement of the personal achievement will usually be attained —but it must not surpass the limitations set by the group monopoly or else these must be re-adjusted. In the second case, when competition within the group has been ruled out, the existing chances will be distributed according to rigid rules. For instance, certain consumers will be consigned to certain producers and the profit will be guaranteed according to a certain fixed percentage. In this case, the closed group approaches the type of a bureaucracy.

CHAPTER VII

F. Selection

Every kind of competition and struggle among masses of people leads to a selection of those who have the abilities which are necessary for survival under the given conditions of a free competition. It would be wrong to believe that struggle and social competition always foster and select those who are the best according to an absolute standard of worth. Selection only fosters those qualities and human abilities which correspond to those social tasks and the social conditions in which competition takes place. In war the struggle may select those who are strongest in a physical sense, who are the most efficient among the cruel conditions of fighting. Competition in an election campaign may foster those who have the greatest ability in creating slogans and propagating them with a loud voice. Competition in a special market may select those who are most unscrupulous. Competition within a bureaucracy, or even within the artistic and scientific world, may put those at a premium who are best at pulling strings and discovering influential patrons.

It is very important, therefore, to distinguish between those faculties which are needed for the objective achievement necessary in a society, which may be called the *objective abilities*, and those capacities which are needed to get one's work or personality accepted and acknowledged: these we might call *social abilities*.

Every personal success is built upon the basis of these two kinds of abilities. The successful man who makes his way alone by objective achievement is very rare; he usually needs certain qualities which help him to convince and impress his fellow beings. On the other hand, it is very seldom that social qualities alone without any real achievement lead to success in a field where free social competition rules. It would be very interesting to map out those social abilities and those objective abilities which make for success in the various professions, the branches of business, or the different social strata. Cooley tried to discover those general qualities which are necessary for the attainment of success in any field. He stressed the importance of five qualities: self control, enterprise, perseverance, address and common sense.

Self control. This quality implies steadiness, the power to subordinate passing impulses to a rational rule. Steadiness is a prime command in every social career. It is also a condition of performing work of a standard quality.

Enterprise. By enterprise Cooley understands the disposition to make experiments on life, to try and try again, which, of course, implies a certain degree of aggressiveness. Enterprise means being in the habit of making, so to say, voyages of discovery in order to find out one's proper relations to the world and to find out where opportunities open.

Perseverance. In times of doubt, discouragement has to be overcome. If you overcome lassitude, depression and discouragement, you have perseverance. The inner ambition of reaching a high standard must be organically connected with social ambition. Mental ambitions wholly detached from social ambitions lead to resentment and feelings of frustration; social ambitions detached from the inner ambition of reaching high standards bring about a personality dominated by vanity.

Address. This quality, according to Cooley, is based on sympathetic insight into human nature, guided by intelligence and steadied by coolness. 'It is a faculty that is necessary to everyone in the early part of his career or at times of change in order to make his way through the social medium to the place where he can bring his special abilities into play.'

Common sense. This quality is based on a humanised and symmetrical intelligence and on a just equilibrium of the finer faculties.

Does competition function like a sieve or like a stamping machine? In the first case the individual himself would not be moulded by the selective process, he would only be selected by it and it would depend on the shape of the 'holes of the sieve' which individuals got through the selective agencies and which did not. But if the selective process is like a stamping machine, the selection actively transforms the individual, urges him to use his innate capacities in a definite way. For example, if you talk to a leading personality in a certain branch of industry or of politics in which forceful people are needed, you will notice that he had probably adapted himself to his job by systematically repressing his sympathetic tendencies, otherwise he would be in danger of being ruled out as being temperamentally unsuited to the work. This is an example where the selective agency acts as a stamping machine and not as a sieve. People who possess the qualities necessary for a ruling group are either moulded through 'the stamping machine process' or selected by 'the sieve process' for leading posts. Usually such people bear signs of having been affected by both 'processes', though one or the other is dominant.

G. The Main Effect of Competition and Selection on Mental Life

It is competition and selection that decide which human types, which standards, which thought patterns will be dominant in a given society.

After the victory of national socialism in Germany, many people were astonished that 'the Germans have changed their minds in such a short time'. People who speak in such terms are far from being able to make a proper sociological analysis. Not all Germans changed their minds between 1930 and 1933, but in the very same society different methods of social selection, brought about by competition and struggle, drew out different types of people. If types which were formerly at the bottom of society reach the top of social scales, their ways of thinking and behaving, formerly insignificant, pass for the new prototype of behaviour. Thereupon propaganda and social imitation help to spread this new type of behaviour and this mental pattern. That is the way in which new Germans were being shaped in a short time. Not the same Germans changed, but the selection favoured a new type which later reacted even upon the older type. It is the same mechanism which brings about a change both in mental patterns and in attitudes. It is not the ideas and the thought patterns which compete with one another, but the individuals. With the rise of a new type of individual, a new set of ideas comes to the top.

Competition and selection have two main effects on social life. First, they dissolve every type of isolation and close group-integration. The isolation and exclusiveness of local units (like farms or villages) change when they begin to participate in the great process of industrial, commercial and political competition. All the symptoms

88

of isolation and many of the habits of stabilised traditional mentality are ruled out in a short time. Second,
although competition dissolves the former stable stratification of a society, it tends at the same time to create a
new stratification. One of the results of an intensive selection is the segregation of the weak. In the slums of great
cities, for instance, we find those segregated who were the
unfittest from the standpoint of a certain selection; for
example, people lacking incentive and activity, the
feeble-minded, but also those who were too soft-hearted
and sentimental to maintain themselves in the struggle for
existence; or those who were born there with an unequal
chance in the social selection which is always in process.

The segregated group in turn again becomes isolated
and soon unfolds its own mentality: the effects of isolation
are again at work.

H. Co-operation and the Division
of Labour

Whereas competition is a force which compels people to
act against one another, co-operation is an integrating
activity. Like-mindedness, sympathy, mutual helpfulness
are the most important integrating forces. Like-mindedness alone does not integrate people for a long period. If
you want to stabilise the integration you must have a
common external purpose.

1. THE PURPOSES OF CO-OPERATION

The most ancient and frequent motive of union has been
co-operation in fighting the enemy. Here two kinds of integration can be distinguished: fighting co-operation can
be based on attack, but can also be based on defence. For

89

instance, the predatory invasions of migrating nomads drew them into large loose unions. Somewhat similar was the union of the Israelites when they made their way into the land of Canaan. Such unions are, of course, temporary, because attack is usually optional. On the other hand, defence is imperative and creates therefore more lasting unions. The fear of being attacked by a powerful enemy is the master-builder of big, permanent unions. It was not the conquest of the land of Canaan which welded the tribes of Israel into a kingdom under Saul and David, but it was their wars with the neighbouring peoples. Another example is furnished by the rise of the Italian mercantile city states in medieval times. Genoa or Venice came into being chiefly in order to protect their trade from piracy and to maintain so-called consuls in the Levant who had the task of looking after their commercial interests.

A further important motive for co-operation was, in the early periods of history, the need to control the waters of great rivers. The early appearance of the despotic states of the Nile, of the Euphrates and of the Ganges, sprang from the necessity of maintaining irrigation ditches and reservoirs.

Another common enterprise is the construction of public works. The early city builders in Babylonia were tillers of the soil who provided themselves primarily with a stronghold and only secondarily with a market place. The essential instrument of such a sheltering stronghold was, of course, the wall.

Economic co-operation, particularly under primitive conditions, does not lead to large groups but gives rise to an infinity of small undertakings, such as the collective hunting of gregarious animals like the buffalo or the hunting of formidable animals like the elephant or the whale, or the providing of common protection for herds against predatory beasts, or the common mowing of the meadows owned by the village community.

Religious worship developed into a community affair rather early in history. It seems that the primitive agricultural tribes felt insecure unless the gods who were supposed to make their crops thrive became established as the permanent and principal members of the community. Hence, the covenant by which in return for the care of its interests, the tribe undertook to maintain for the gods, temples, and to organise regular sacrifices and worship. The domestication of their gods helped to train the primitive people for combined action.

That mutual aid is possible in certain circumstances without the help of sanctions based upon force, is shown by the voluntary establishment of tribunals for the settlement of disputes. The creation of the Icelandic republic in the tenth century is an instance of the possibility of settling disputes peacefully. The inhabitants of small settlements on this island organised a Republic in order to provide a machinery which would put an end to the feuds which raged among them. A government was established without an executive side. Only its judicial and legislative functions had developed. The League of Nations was in some respects a similar instrument: a voluntary, co-operative authority. The question can be asked, with some justification, whether it was not the absence of an international police force which was the main cause of the failure of the League. Further questions may be asked in connection with plans for a universal league of states. Can an international peaceful integration last for a long time, without the existence of an external opponent? Do we always need an external enemy in order to get a permanent peaceful internal integration? Is it necessary for a world wide integration to have an external enemy something like a threat coming from the inhabitants of Mars? Can the danger inherent in the huge accumulation of the instruments of war function as well as the threats of an external enemy as a lasting integrating force?

2. CO-OPERATION, COMPULSION AND MUTUAL AID

Co-operation cannot be effected without some kind of compulsion. The simplest forms of compulsion are needs arising from the dangers inherent in the forces of nature. The anarchists err in deriding coercive authority as the child of conquest or of personal ambition.

The most spontaneous co-operation between groups is the mutual aid between neighbours, which is a spontaneous combination of efforts without submission to authority. The characteristic of this spontaneous readiness to give mutual aid, is that it works better in hard times than in easy times. Many examples can be found for this: merchants band themselves into guilds when they are striving for recognition by kings or priests or when they are threatened by robbers; artisans organise themselves when they are struggling for legal rights; wage earners form unions to defend their economic rights and to improve conditions of work; settlers practise mutual aid, especially when they are poor and struggling. So, for instance, among the pioneers of North America it was customary that if a man was sick his neighbours would offer to harvest his crop. But also when all were well they used to 'exchange work' in harvest times. In a later period when most members of the pioneering communities were better off, these mutual aid customs became less usual.

Generally speaking the lower social classes are more in favour of mutual aid than the middle or the upper classes. The explanation for this is that in hard times most people realise how essential are the principles of co-operation, mutual aid, the principles of *do ut des*.

Mutual help is a response to social pressure which can often be observed in history. For example, the labouring folk of ancient Rome bound themselves together in so-called *collegia*. There was a union for each trade to protect its members against the upper classes, to assure security in work and to lend some dignity to existence. Each had its festivals and sacred banquets, its banners, its common fund, its elected head and its common property in building and land. Christianity, the religion of love and of brotherly aid, captured this class long before it won the high and proud.

According to Kropotkin, the Slavonic ideal has always been the group of small producers, the members of which were co-operating with one another, rather than the vast industrial concern, exercising an autocratic control over their personnel. There is some truth in the assertion that people who have but recently emerged from their old communal organisation, like the Slavs or the peoples of Asia, still preserve a set of spontaneous co-operative tendencies. In the bigger cities, on the other hand, the sense of mutual aid tends to disappear. The voluntary method of taking care of common needs is little used then—the community has become too large for its members to know each other personally and to act readily in concert. The community has become so differentiated that the sense of common needs to be cared for commonly has been dulled.

3. THE SOCIAL FUNCTION OF THE DIVISION OF LABOUR

We distinguish between simple collaboration, co-operation which is based upon a division of functions and co-operation which is based upon a division of professions.

As an example of simple collaboration we can mention common wood-cutting by the members of a village community. In such an operation, everybody can share in the performance of the common task without the need for a definite division of functions having to arise.

As a type of a definite division of functions but without professionalisation, the division of labour in primitive communities based upon sex itself can be cited. In this case men may go hunting and prepare for the task of fighting, whilst the women do agricultural work or prepare the meals.

Definite professions are formed when different groups of individuals deal with one task only. This is a higher form of specialization. Some individuals may become fishermen, living in the vicinity of rivers, others, living in the mountains, may become herdsmen, while the dwellers of the plain specialise in agriculture and become farmers. Miners and armourers or smiths are among the earliest specialists, making up the first professions.

The main factor responsible for the division of labour is obviously the greater efficiency of labour organised in this way. There is the familiar example given by Adam Smith of the needle manufacturing process. According to him, as an effect of the division of labour, eighteen workers were producing in one instance 200 times as much as they would have produced working separately without a division of labour. Adam Smith was convinced that the reason for the division of labour taking place was always an exchange of products undertaken between producers. He assumed that producers concentrated on the production of one part of a whole project in order to be able to exchange it. In his view, it was the utilitarian calculation of the single individual which urged him to differentiate his work. He was mistaken in that he considered as the main working incentive that which was dominant in a liberal society. To-day we know that the division of labour is older than profitable exchange. There is a division of labour in societies where there is no exchange at all. There are many tribes which know a system of division of labour but disdain bartering. Goods are never exchanged among them, they move from one man to another either as presents or by being stolen.

The different stages in the evolution of the division of labour can best be followed in connection with the different typical stages in the evolution and growth of the co-operative units.

The first stage in this evolution is the family or the family-like domestic and economic unit ('economics' derives from a root meaning 'the art of the house or the household'). This unit is a more or less self-sufficient autarkic community which produces most of the things which it needs. Everybody produces for the needs of all. Exchange may take place but is rare. Even the early medieval manor fits more or less into this type.

The second type is the economy of the small town, where the small workshops of the handicraft men were based upon a highly developed division of labour. This division of labour implies a product which can be split up into component parts, but the control of the final product remains, from beginning to end, in the hands of the same producer, who usually manufactures it for definite consumers. This system, although based upon professionalisation, is hostile to specialisation. It prevents a decomposition of the object so that parts might be made in different places, and it is also a check upon a rapid increase of personal wealth; whilst on the other hand it usually functions in such a way as to prevent pauperisation.

If the consumer or the merchant brings raw material directly to the artisan and gives orders to him, the process of decomposition has been pushed a step further. Under more developed circumstances the differentiation of labour may be guided more by market exchange. But differentiation by organisation is a permanent factor of the division of labour.

As a third type of economy Bücher contrasted with domestic economy and city economy, the system of national economy. In this system, the various branches of industry procure their raw materials themselves, they produce for an unknown buyer and do not wait for immediate orders; the commodities thus produced circulate

95

in the whole society. Bücher also speaks of the stage of world economy where the market shows an extension over the whole surface of the globe and in which large scale industry concentrates production and organises the division of labour. The speculation of the capital owners driven by the profit incentive, decides upon capital investments and contributes to the development of trade cycles. Planned (or managed) economy seems to be the last stage in this picture of the evolution of the systems of production, division of labour and of exchange. However, this suggested sequence can only be regarded as a useful tool for investigating different types of economy, but not as a rigid system of development in the actual historical process.

4. THE SOCIAL VALUATION OF LABOUR

The distinction between 'noble' and 'ordinary' professions, reappears in social history again and again: in patriarchal societies, especially in the later stage of development, it is common to emphasise the noble character of the work of the warrior and of the hunter. Agricultural work is usually performed by slaves and women and this work is underestimated, although it may be much more difficult and harder work than hunting or taking part in war-like raids. This instance seems to prove that the social valuation of work does not coincide with its usefulness to the community, but hinges more upon the power structure of that society and on the fact that some functions are reserved for the ruling groups and others are allotted to the subjected ones. The work done by small artisans and handicraft men, being very similar to that of the work done by slaves, was not highly esteemed in the city states of Greece. Manual work was conceived in antiquity as corrupting both the body and the soul. Even the work of the sculptor and of the architect was looked down upon for many centuries, because the members of these professions originally came from the slave stratum and because the professions entailed manual work. The poet, on the other hand, who historically descended from the soothsayer or oracle, was held in high esteem.

On a higher stage of social differentiation, the nobles of the community connect the idea of noble work with the idea of leisure. According to their view only the man who has leisure and is able to contribute his share to the administration of the community, by taking over political or other communal functions without being paid for it, does 'noble' work. Both in Rome and in England administrative work was done for centuries on a voluntary basis by the members of the aristocracy—and only this unpaid work was considered to be worthy of a noble man.

In the rising democratic times, on the other hand, a counter-ideal was conceived: that of the nobility of *all* socially useful work. In Athens, in the democratic period, it was not regarded as shameful to be a descendant of a family of handicraft men, as was the case with such influential leaders as Cleon or Demosthenes.

In the early stages of our own European society, making war, hunting, the service of the king and voluntary service within the bureaucracy were considered as noble work. Later, leading functions in agriculture were also highly esteemed, but industrial and commercial functions were looked down upon. With the growth of the influence and wealth of the industrial and commercial middle classes, the so-called bourgeoisie, successful work in finance, commerce and industry began to be respected. Finally, during the nineteenth century, the century during which the ideals of democracy and socialism gained strong influence, the original scale of valuations was turned into its opposite, since sometimes there was a tendency to over-estimate manual work and to under-rate the significance of other kinds of work. For many members of our society, only manual work seems to be productive.

7—S.S. 97

From this example we can observe clearly that social position, the rise and fall of various groups in a society, influences strongly the fundamental standards underlying our judgment of value.

5. THE INTEGRATING FUNCTION OF THE DIVISION OF LABOUR

Besides leading to greater productivity, division of labour has another very important effect—as an integrating factor. This was first described by the French sociologist Durkheim. At first sight, division of labour seems to be a separating agency. But if we realise that every division of labour divides the activities, which were formerly combined in a process of work performed by one man, into a great number of parts which are supplementary to each other, then we must realise that division of labour means that the work of one man or group seeks completion in that of another. Consequently, the division of labour must lead to the strongest kind of social integration. It is the strongest kind because it is a *functional* integration. The connection of functions and the exchange of services is the essence of the process.

Completing this observation, Durkheim distinguishes two kinds of social integration and two types of solidarity. First, *the mechanical solidarity of likeness* which rests upon the total subjection of the individual to the group. The group in question is called by Durkheim the unisegmentary or monosegmentary group. Second, *organic solidarity*, which rests upon social differentiation, a system in which one organ supplements the functions of the other. According to Durkheim the division of labour is due very often to the great density of population. If huge masses are concentrated in cities—as in the west—and not so widely spread as they were, for instance, in Russia and China in past centuries, the conditions are favourable for the developing of the process of the division of labour. It is interesting that the working of a similar law can be observed already in animal and plant life: homogeneous plants or animals cannot survive in some territories except in small numbers, but divergent races, if united on a similar territory, thrive in great numbers. The conditions urge them to a specialisation of functions. A similar result can be found in the fusion of small groups.

To the two kinds of solidarity, the mechanical and the organic, two kinds of morality seem to belong: (1) Uni-segmentary society is based upon mechanical imitation and rigid traditions. It does not tolerate deviations. (2) The more complex society of our day requires individual deviations because the various differentiated functions of this society can only be fulfilled by various individualised types.

PART 3

SOCIAL INTEGRATION

CHAPTER VIII

A. The Sociology of Groups

So far I have considered general social forces and processes which either bring people together (these are
the integrating forces) or urge them to act against
one another (these are the separating forces). But I have
not yet dealt with the end-products of these forces, with
the various possible forms of integration, with the groups
which are nothing but the more or less stabilised results
of the general social processes.

The great mistake of every kind of lay sociology is that
it considers such units as a political party, a family, a
business corporation, a church or state as a sort of
mythical entity, that is to say, as a substantial unit, and
fails to realise that these units are nothing but the integrations of diverse forces and tendencies. The reason
why the description of single forces has to precede in
sociology the theory of the group, is that without such a
description we cannot analyse and break up these mythical entities into their elements. It is our task now to
observe here, one by one, the different stages of social
integration and the different forms of more or less compact and stable social groups.

1. THE CROWD

I shall start with a marginal case, with that kind of social
integration which has the loosest structure. This is *the
crowd.*

If you observe people on a Sunday in Hyde Park, you

will have before you a mass possessing no integration whatsoever. But what happens if the attention of these people is focussed by an accident or if they begin to participate in a riot? The form of their integration is not then based so much on the fact that they react upon each other like members of a small group of friends, or a working group, as by the fact that they react to the same stimuli. One might say that they have similar interests and their responses are being made more or less uniform by being conditioned by the same stimuli. This is a description of a passive mass, but let a fire have to be put out by the members of this crowd—then the mass undergoes a change, it begins to become organised, though it is not easy for a random crowd to develop the disciplined and co-ordinated action of a purposive group, for such a group has a period of training and adaptation behind it. However, in so far as the crowd tries to deal with the fire an important change has occurred because there are now common activating interests.

The crowd may be defined as a physical, compact aggregation of human beings brought into direct, temporary and unorganised contact, reacting mostly to the same stimuli and in a similar way. It is always a transitory and unstable organisation, an incident, an eruption; therefore, integration based upon immediate suggestion plays an important part. All the inhibitions maintained by primary and organised groups tend to lose their strength in a crowd and the consequence is that a sudden regression to primary, primitive, uncontrolled reaction can occur very easily. Under such conditions, the sudden communication and accumulation of emotion creates a loss of the sense of responsibility and maybe even of identity. This loss leads to an overthrowing of the standards and habits which formerly were developed within the framework of enduring groups.

In the crowd the close physical contacts, the multitudinous swaying emotions, the gestures, the murmurs and

104

shouts, stir deep-laid strivings and the symptoms of the crowd become intensified when a like interest is turned into a common interest. For instance, the group which at the beginning of the French Revolution stormed the Bastille was a like-interest group and not a crowd of passive observers. They were united by a revolutionary aim. In such a situation, such a very simple aim causes each to identify himself with all the rest. This sort of participation brings with it a social sanction for individual irresponsibility. It is here that the function of the leader enters the plan. The leader becomes a means of identification, he is henceforth the symbol of this group, of group identification, of group organisation. He is followed, not because he has social prestige or a certain status, as would happen in conservative societies or in times of a continuous evolution, but because the rank and file has faith in him.

The unorganised crowd is usually subjected to a process in which emotion increases and the capacity for reflection is lowered. In this stage nothing constructive can be done, because there is no common end. The crowd is then in a transitory stage, it preserves the material for integration, it is, so to say, susceptible to the reformation of new, consolidated groups, a solidarity which could replace the centrifugal tendencies potentially present.

The crowd often seeks for a victim, such as the aristocrats or the Jews. In such a crowd the personal censor is removed, and the primitive or infantile nature of man reappears. Emotion is prominent in such a crowd and it seems as if the repressed aggressive and sexual tendencies would take their revenge. The skilful politician, the evangelist, the patriot of our times, the tribal witchdoctor, all use methods which are within limits similar, directing the crowd by voice and gesture, by reiteration and the cumulation of images, by all the ingredients of the spell of the orator.

The crowd exhibits the underlying gregarious spirit in the processes of social integration, and modern techniques of communication create new avenues for that kind of spirit. The press or the radio thus may become agencies for the transmission of this gregariousness.

2. THE PUBLIC

The public is an integration of many people not based on personal interaction but on reaction to the same stimuli —a reaction arising without the members of the public necessarily being physically near to one another.

What are the significant features of an agglomeration of people who are attending a football match, watching the performance of a play or listening to an orator? The significant features here are that there is a great number of people assembled, that they are near to each other and that they make their responses not to one another but to the same stimuli. They are actually integrated only by the purpose of being affected by certain stimuli (in the game, the play, the speaker and his words) and reacting to these. Nevertheless, they are no longer a crowd but can be called a public, first of all because their integration is more or less purposive—they came in order to listen to the orator or to watch the game; secondly, a primary kind of organisation, an external routine of timetable and behaviour, stands behind them: they have certain seats, they occupy and leave their seats at definite times, etc. Finally, they play the definite role of being observers, of being an audience and they have the right to applaud or to criticise.

Observing a public, we can note from the common experience of their members that a certain kind of group spirit emerges spontaneously, based mainly on commonly experienced and expressed moods and emotions. These experiences and emotions are often guided and the climax, the integration and disintegration of these, takes place simultaneously in the whole agglomeration of people. As a result of these common experiences, we can even speak here of the development of a short, common tradition of the members of the public.

There is a further factor which distinguishes the public from the crowd. Namely, that certain elementary forms of public opinion also arise. Thus we see that during the pauses, small groups are formed by certain initiating personalities. Members of the public who go from one group to another influence the selection and launching of opinions. The public is for a time divided into active and passive elements. This is a differentiation of functions, but these functions are fluctuating and interchangeable. We can observe the transition from the public to a group if its members begin to react to one another, if reflectiveness arises in its members and if the individualised personality begins to play a greater role. The public is thus an intermediate type of integration between the crowd and the group.

3. ABSTRACT MASSES AND THE ABSTRACT PUBLIC

People who listen on the radio in various parts of the country to the same play or to the same speech or who look at the same advertisement in different streets or read the same leading article in their newspapers or read the same novel at home, form abstract masses or an abstract public. They form a mass because the unity of these people is formed only by the common reaction to the same stimuli; not the whole personality is engaged in listening to the wireless or reading a novel, but only a part of it. But the readers or the radio listeners do not form a crowd because all the reactions connected with physical, bodily presence are absent. They are a public because they follow the same experiences. The functions to approve or to reject, that is, to judge the value of the

107

performance or of the novel, are maintained and these functions are fluctuating. The decisive fact is that as members of an abstract public we behave according to social integration. If we react to an advertisement, we react in some measure as the members of a crowd would react to a suggestion, we are thus members of an abstract crowd; if we react to the leading article of a newspaper, we react as members of an abstract public. The advertisement and the article are constructed with these factors in mind.

Every member of a society is in an ambiguous situation: as the member of a family or of a party he is influenced by certain definite types of motivation. Thus he has political attitudes, aesthetic attitudes, family feelings, sex attitudes, and so on. But if he becomes for a short time the member of a public in a real sense, he puts his traditionalised attitudes into brackets and lets himself be influenced by the impressions of the attitudes of a public. For instance, if a member of the Communist party is listening to the lecture of a Liberal on the problem of the freedom of the press, he must, if he wishes really to become a member of the listening public, put the traditional attitudes of his party into brackets. If he does not do so, he does not become a part of the new, momentary integration of the public except as a critical and separated member, and his fixed group attitude prevails. The public is the ever-present fluid element alongside the consolidated groupings.

On the other hand, as long as the fluctuating impulses of the public do not become organised and transformed into traditional group attitudes, they react upon the individual mind but do not transform the existing society. The totality of a society can only be explained in terms of both the fluid integrations and the group consolidations. We see here a balance between public spirit and group spirit. Fluid public opinion is the guarantee of the dynamic and flexible spirit of modern times as we can observe it in most parts of Europe since the time of the Renaissance.

Freedom of thought, sociologically, means that a person can think not only in terms of his organised group patterns but also in terms of the flexible reactions to the more fluid integrations of various abstract publics. The abolition of the freedom of thought in modern dictatorial society consists not simply in forbidding people to think, but in organising, and thereby making rigid, the public, which is in its essence an unorganised entity and can only function properly if it remains unorganised and fluid.

4. ORGANISED GROUPS

These are the more or less enduring forms of the social integration of a certain number of people who react according to a certain set of social forces. They react not only to external stimuli but to one another. The main characteristics of groups are:

(*a*) A relative persistence.

(*b*) Organisation, that is, a certain degree of division of functions.

(*c*) Social institutions based on certain traditional habits of the individuals composing the groups.

(*d*) Certain group norms or standards to which the members of the group adjust their activities.

(*e*) Certain ideas about the existence and the functions of the group and its relationships to other groups. Subjective ideas of the members of the group on its destiny and function do not, in many cases, coincide with its real functions in society. In such cases we can speak about the ideologies of the group members. The knowledge of these ideologies is very important because it helps to explain the activities of the groups. They can be regarded as parts of a defence mechanism, a kind of rationalisation or unwitting falsification, necessary for the successful functioning of the group. For instance, the members of a political party think that the purpose of their party is to help the economically weaker sections of the middle classes. Nevertheless, another function of the group, in realistic terms, may be to support and defend the ruling groups to retain their power and privileges. The criterion of the realistic functions can be found not in the words of the members of a group, or in the written programme but in the deeds.

(*f*) Every group has a collective interest and, at the same time, every member of the group has a personal and a collective interest in it.

(*g*) Every group has a more or less developed power organisation and a system of distribution of power.

(*k*) Every group produces specific situations, with typical tensions, repressions and conflicts, as well as typical repressive and discharging agencies.

Examples of groups are the family, the clan, the tribe, the neighbourhood community, the church, the sect, the political party, the bureaucracy and the state.

Observing the life of these groups in the course of history or their functioning in contemporary society, we see that they are knit together firstly by like responses, habits, social institutions; secondly, by complementary functions; thirdly, by fixed organisation and fourthly by conscious elements, such as norms, interests and ideologies.

The simplest forms of group integration are collective attitudes which fall into two groups: those which are relatively permanent—these we call institutional attitudes; and those which are comparatively ephemeral and change their character rapidly—the non-institutional attitudes.

Customs are examples of institutional attitudes, being uniformities of behaviour which tend to form habits in the individual. They come down from past generations, sometimes from periods so remote that it is impossible to trace their origin. The main holidays and festivals of any modern church have their origin in most cases in very ancient celebrations, and traditions are the psychic aspects of custom. However, practices are more easily imitated than ideas.

Folkways are uniform ways of doing things within a group; doing things for instance in the fields of recreation, social contacts or economic life. But the more settled forms of social contact, such as religion or public ceremonies, do not belong to this group. Conventions are simply present ways of doing things or contemporaneous beliefs about things. Conventional people are those who do not like to depart from the accepted forms of action and thought, and codes of conduct are laid down and formally sanctioned by some approving body which possesses authority for the sake of definiteness.

Non-institutional controls can be observed in connection with such social phenomena as the fad, the fashion or the craze. These are forms of behaviour which are not very widespread and which pass relatively quickly, a form of behaviour in the matter of speech, recreation, cooking, dress, or the like.

When we join a group, the process of becoming uniform starts at once. The consequence of this process of becoming uniform can best be observed in the case of professional groups in which professionalisation creates the same type again and again. It is partly the nature of the work but to a greater extent the imitation of and the adaptation to the standards of the profession which make members of a profession similar to one another. Groups consisting of two or three persons do not need group norms, as they represent purely personal relationships. The larger the group, the more must the personal attitudes be transformed into stereotyped standards and patterns. Group norms are, of course, not abstract rules but visible patterns or types of behaviour and attitude. Thus a living or a dead person can become the model for the members of a group.

CHAPTER IX

The Sociology of Groups *(continued)*

5. THE TYPES OF GROUPINGS

According to Simmel, very much depends in a group on the number of participants. There are basic differences in the nature of groups formed of two, three, four or a multitude of persons.

First, we must deal with small groups; these we may call quasi-groups. The smallest of these is the couple. We know sex couples formed by a man and a woman who may be lovers or married couples. But couples are also formed by members of different generations, like father and son or mother and daughter, and also by members of the same generation—brother and sister. We see couples based on friendship or based on subordination (employer and employee, teacher and student). Transitory contacts do not create groups, only constant relationship does so, and therefore we deal here with the latter only.

The couple relationship is the most intensive group relationship because the whole personality can enter into it. Most intensive relationships into which love and friendship enter seem to be correlated with the group termed couple. It is the social form most adapted to a specific intimacy. The personal quality of the members is more important in the couple than in large size groups. This is quite obvious in the case of friendship couples and the humanising of the couple relationship is the essential of friendship: in the couple the personal self becomes distinguishable from the social self.

The couple reacts on external stimuli differently from

the way in which individuals constituting the couple would act, separately. This is so because the members of the couple have a more or less permanent influence on each other. On the other hand, the less individualised the members of a couple are, the easier though not necessarily the richer is its functioning.

The next group with which we must deal is the group with three members. This group can be regarded as an extension of the couple but, of course, the appearance of a third member alters the whole balance between the members of the couple. The attitude of the original group, the couple, towards the third, who approaches the group, must also be taken into consideration when we analyse the nature of the new group. The consequence for the third member of the group may be temporary isolation, which lasts until he finds a new partner. A typical symptom of behaviour in a group of three is jealousy. The competition of two people for the favour of a third is very characteristic of many three-person relationships.

The layman usually tends to believe that the behaviour of man is more constant than it really is. The study of small groups shows very convincingly that he is wrong. The behaviour of persons changes according to changing circumstances. Thus, every meeting of two persons is influenced by such factors as what each feels about the other, what he seems to feel about me, the personal mood of myself but also of the other whom I meet, the occasion and purpose of our meeting and all the other factors conditioning this meeting.

There exists no definite and exclusive classification of social groups. All classifications depend on the nature of the point of view according to which way the variety of objects in question is considered. The usefulness or unfitness of a classification depends both on the purposes of the scientific observation and on the nature of the object itself. That is the reason why I offer various kinds of classifications of social groupings.

We have to distinguish purely statistical groups from sociological units. By a purely statistical group we understand a group of people having the same characteristics, who are united into a group in the mind of a scholar or statistician only, without being really integrated on the basis of these characteristics. Purely statistical groups are, for instance, 'males', 'females', 'newborns', 'redheads', '30-year-olds', 'agricultural labourers'. Our problem here is whether their common traits act as real group makers or not. The difficulty in applying statistics is that in statistics we need measurable units and therefore external characteristics have to be found. The nature of the real social bond on the other hand is mostly a psychological-spiritual one. People rarely act together on the basis of external features but very often on the basis of common psychological stimuli. When the statistical classification corresponds to a social or psychological bond, the data obtained may have considerable value in helping us to understand social processes, as can be seen when we consider income groups, ethnic or religious minority groups or the like.

Groups were classified by Tönnies into *communities* and *associations*. A community can be defined as any circle of people who live together and belong together in such a way that they do not share this or that particular interest only, but a whole set of interests. A community is a group which is wide enough to include, so to say, the whole life of its members. Such groups are the tribe, the village, the pioneer settlement, the city and the nation, but not the business firm, the professional organisation or the typical political party. The mark of a community is that one's life may be lived wholly within it.

A community is a social group occupying a territorial area and the common locality has an important part in creating its social coherence. But a purely spatial unit alone does not constitute the social bond: there must be common living. The fact that we belong to a small community (such as the village) of course does not exclude the possibility that we should adhere to a wider one such as the nation.

An association, on the other hand, is a group specifically organised for the pursuit of an interest or of a group of interests, in common. It is not a community, but an organisation within a community—such as a business firm or a club. If we observe various associations, we can always tell which are the particular interests around which these organisations are formed, but we cannot ask why communities exist, for what purpose, any more than we can ask why life exists.

We belong to an association only by virtue of the purposes of that association; some part of our life always escapes it. We are born into communities, but we choose our associations or are elected into them. Of course, there are many social groupings which are on the borderline between community and association. For instance, the family was formerly a community in the pure sense because it included the whole life of its members. Under modern conditions it tends to become more or less of an association. But, of course, it is still a community in the original sense, for the child.

Blood relationship and local groups. Which common factors act as group makers and which data and traits act as an impetus for common activities and for the emergence of a group consciousness? At different times and in different societies, and even within the same society, group integration often follows different lines. For instance, in nomadic times it was mostly the blood relationship which was the fundamental integrating influence. Family, kinship and tribe are, therefore, in such times and societies the basic factors of integration. All kinds of co-operative and ideological unification serve the aim of strengthening this classification. The totem expresses symbolically the form of this synthesis. But once a group of people gets settled, an element of space enters into the social relationship and local groupings become more important than blood relationship. Under settled circumstances people who live in the same village form a local community. It is significant that the immigrant, who settles down, or more significantly, is allowed to settle down, in the village, even if he does not belong to the kinship, may become a member of the local community.

At first, there is usually a struggle and competition between these two kinds of primary integrating principles and much depends on whether, during decisive periods of history, the tribal or the local integration prevails. In old Russia and in China the tribal organisation prevailed for a long time. The Russian peasant of the last century belonged to the *mir* and did not lose his adherence to it even when he went to town. If, however, the local unit prevails, the symptom of this change is usually that the tribal deity is replaced by a local deity, and there are instances of both forms of integration occurring together.

To-day, in our society, the principle of local unification still functions, although it is balanced by other principles of integration. The state is to-day the most impressive territorial community, based upon an integration bringing together many aspects of living together. But such primary groups, based on blood-relationship or local unification, as the family, the neighbourhood, the playground, also have their function, as Cooley has shown us. However, besides the principles of blood relationship and locality there are many other principles on which group integration may be based.

The principle of common activities gives rise to the professional groups. These arise because similar activities urge people to stand together. Here we have to distinguish two stages: in the first stage, groups are built upon spontaneous co-operation and in the second stage, there is set up an organisation with the purpose of knitting the different parts of the group together. By an organisation we mean a kind of co-operation in which the functions of every part of the group are definitely pre-arranged and stated and in which there is a guarantee that the planned activities and demands will be executed without major frictions. The best example of a group based upon common activities in connection with a strict organisation is a bureaucracy, that is, the executing organ of a state, of a business, of a party or of a trade union.

The principle of fighting for power within the state gives rise to political parties. There is always a process of re-distribution and re-organisation of power going on in the state and the agents in this conflict are the political parties. The nature and functioning of these can only be understood if we introduce the distinction between direct activities and representative activities. Under the latter we understand acting on behalf of somebody else. The necessity of introducing representatives gives rise to various difficulties. The representative may act in a manner not satisfactory to those whom he represents, he may go beyond his brief. It will, therefore, be necessary to build up a mechanism in order to readjust, if necessary, the personal will of the representative to the will of the mandating persons. The problem of what the common will of a group is and how it can be measured and expressed, gives rise to further problems connected with such procedures as elections, the functioning of oppositions, the protection of the rights of minorities, and so on. Parliaments, councils, congresses, are means of organising the will of a group for the sake both of giving initiative to and controlling the executive.

The principle of defending common interests gives rise to a grouping together of associations of employers, or of the trade unions, or the like. The membership of these associations is limited to a definite circle of persons. But the groupings based upon a general rather than a specific likeness and upon the free choice of companions have a different basis of recruitment. We have here selective associations founded on the principle of the free choice of companions and such are common experience groups or groups wishing to spend their leisure time together.

The principle of groups based upon free choice gives rise to innumerable free associations. There is no space to deal with all of them. I would like only to mention that many religious groups belong here although the religious aim (as all other aims) may be linked up with common interests and with the striving for common power.

6. THE STATE

One form of group must be discussed apart from the groups so far mentioned: this is the frame-group and in our epoch the frame-group is the state.

The frame-group is the power organisation which acquires the greatest control among existing groupings within a territory and is able to regulate the interrelations between all other fighting, competing or co-operating groups. The modern state has the power and claims the right to interfere more or less decisively in many of the relationships binding together all the other groups. The representatives of the state claim this right on the basis of the idea of legitimacy. The idea of legitimacy is a notion which governs the activities of the members of a state as long as the state is really acknowledged by them. The basis of legitimacy may differ in different states; it may be based upon traditional belief, upon established law or upon consent as expressed in plebiscites or elections. The idea of legitimacy differentiates the coercion as used by the state from the coercion used by a gang of robbers. The majority of people do not feel that the coercion exerted by robbers, even if one has to submit to it, is legitimate. The coercion of the state may be felt, subjectively, by many people as illegitimate, but as long as it succeeds in compelling people to act according to the rules laid down by the state, it has to be considered as legitimate *de facto*. The existence of a *de facto* legitimate state can be inferred from the fact that the orders of the state claiming legitimacy have, in fact, the chance of being executed.

The idea of legitimacy *de facto* can mean that a few groups may obtain and maintain power in order to suppress all others. As long as the majority of the population acts in such a way as to show its respect for or submission to the frame-group and thus acknowledges its authority and legitimacy, the frame-group, however oppressive, is the *de facto* state.

Even the individuals who do not acknowledge the legitimacy of the existing state show by their attitudes that they acknowledge the real existence of the state. For instance, the thief acts against the law, but acknowledges its real existence because he hides his activities. In the same way, the organisers of so-called illegal political activities involuntarily acknowledge the real existence of the state by being compelled to organise their activities with a keen eye to the legal regulations.

During a revolution there exists no such frame-group possessing the monopoly of legitimate coercion. The state disappears and partial bodies acquire parts of the power of the state to coerce. In stable times the power of the state is limited by the power of other states competing with it on the international scene. We have so far no world state. Bodies like the League of Nations or the United Nations may proclaim their right of being the source of supreme legitimacy but as long as such a body has not the coercive power guaranteeing the chance that its orders will be obeyed, it is not the real frame-group of international society.

CHAPTER X

B. The Class Problem

Having dealt with the nature and types of social groups we must now discuss the class problem. Class itself is more a layer than a group. Speaking of classes we must distinguish first social position; then the problem of the integrated class; and finally the political party as an organ of class activities.

1. SOCIAL POSITION

People who have similar positions in the social order have a greater chance of having certain experiences than others. For example, anybody who wears a worn-out coat and boots with holes (features which place him in the hierarchy of the social order) has a greater chance than others of being treated in an unfriendly way and without social reverence. Further, persons who have the same social position have a greater chance of responding to certain events and stimuli in a similar way. There is a chance that the philosophies of life of people having the same social position will correspond to some extent because of the experiences they have in common.

What is the difference between a class and a layer? The similarity of persons who belong to a given layer may be based upon various factors such as age, sex, education, etc. People who belong to the same layer have a chance to have similar experiences and may have also similar response patterns in certain fields. Persons belonging to the same generation, for instance, will have some similar experiences in their early childhood or during their adolescence, such as war, unemployment, prosperity, revolution or counter-revolution. Nevertheless, they do not form a class because the similarities which exist among the members of such a layer are not fundamental and consequently do not become integrated.

We can call fundamental such similarities as induce persons to feel alike and to act on the same lines. These similarities are, so to say, the breeding instances of common class activities, and of class consciousness. This set of characteristics can be found firstly in the similarity of chances of getting more or less of the goods which form the wealth of a nation, secondly in the similarity of chances of experiencing the same social respect (often called 'status') and thirdly in the similarity of chances of having comparable careers.

Economic class position, as mentioned above, can be differentiated as class according to possessions and income or class according to relationship to the means of production, as for example owner or employee.

If the *layer* is formed by people who can be characterised by chances of similar experiences, then *class* is the sum of people who find themselves in the same position concerning their fate in society.

Change from one social position, from one class to another, is called vertical mobility. If this vertical mobility is stopped by institutionalised regulations then we say that society is being divided into rigid ranks or castes.

An *integrated* class is the sum of people who are unified not only by these chances but by a class consciousness.

By class consciousness we understand the awareness of the similarity of social chances, the arising of a notion about similarity of interests, the growth of an emotional tie connected with this similarity of experiences and of a common striving towards a common social goal. This common striving is based on a compound of ideal and material interests. Class consciousness is the means by which the spiritual integration of persons possessing a similarity of social position and of life chances is transformed into a common group activity.

2. CLASS CONSCIOUSNESS AND POLITICAL PARTIES

Class consciousness alone does not bring about an acting class; it is only the soil for an easier growth of similar activities, a favourable soil for the development of certain social movements. In order to transform this common background of experiences, of emotional attitudes and of a uniting consciousness into long-term activities, certain social organs of the class must arise; among which the *political parties* are the most important. That is to say, the factor of organisation here enters the plan. We find class parties on the lines of the common activities which correspond to class interests, as defined above. But we find parties on various other lines if there is no definite correspondence between the class background and the rival political parties.

If the owners and the non-owners of the means of production are represented by definite and different parties, then we see the emergence of a party system based on economic class differences. But this does not always happen in the course of history. Which factors tend to bring about such integrations have to be studied in historical sociology. There we study the concrete structures of different societies and this may help us to understand the main trends of integration and their varying intensities.

PART 4

SOCIAL STABILITY AND SOCIAL CHANGE

CHAPTER XI

Factors of Social Stability

Turning to the problem of social structure, we must first study some of those forces which make for social cohesion and stability. These are the so-called social controls, such as custom and law. The problem of authority and of valuations has also to be analysed here and the personal representations of social control and authority have to be defined.

1. SOCIAL CONTROL AND AUTHORITY

What is it that guarantees stability to an existing system? Why do people obey certain rules for their activities? The orderliness and stability of a society is due to the existence of social controls. Social control is the sum of those methods by which a society tries to influence human behaviour to maintain a given order. There are hundreds of controls operating in society but usually their existence passes unnoticed. Every society has a different system of controls, or at least lays emphasis on different controls and controls can be exercised from different key positions. The simplest we may call mutual controls, as for instance when one member of a group rebuffs another for bad behaviour. The control is mutual because it is not yet transferred to an acknowledged agency which exercises control on behalf of the group, such as the police. The different controls are linked up with a system of sanctions, which vary from individual disapprobation on the part of one's fellows, which may be expressed by laughter, cold-shouldering and cutting in the street, to official punishment in the form of fines, imprisonment, etc.

The functioning of control is based upon the existence of authority. There are people of authority, there are statements of authority. There is no social order without authority, but the sources of this authority may be different. The source of authority may be procedure, tradition, established law, or the words of a prophet or a saint. Both anarchists and the supporters of brute force are mistaken, for social order cannot be built up without authority, and authority cannot rest on the threat of violence alone. Most societies are built up on an elaborate system of controls among which physical force is only a last resort. The existing controls are nearly all mutually dependent, and if one is relaxed another will at once replace it. Paternal authority was once the main focus of control, but to-day many of its functions are transferred to the state. To begin with a new kind of behaviour can often only be enforced by rigid control, but later this can be relaxed as habit systems take its place. Out of the many existing controls we will here discuss in detail only custom and law.

2. CUSTOM AS A FORM OF SOCIAL CONTROL

Custom is the earliest form of social control and whereas law is always made and always enforced by a definite power, according to MacIver custom is a group of procedures which has gradually emerged without any constituted authority to declare it and to impose it. In a simple group or in a primitive society mutual controls prevail and there custom is really democratic and totalitarian at the same time. It is democratic because it is made by the group, everybody contributes to its growth, anybody may act upon it and may re-interpret it according to any new situation. It is totalitarian because it affects every sphere of self-expression, private and public, it influences our thoughts, beliefs and manners. Sumner called these relatively durable standardised usages prevailing in a group 'folkways'—for example, the way of building houses, the worship of ancestors, the procedure of initiating members into a secret society, the wearing of clerical vestments and the mannerisms of speech and gesture. Although they vary from one tribe, nation or sect to another, as long as they are the ways of the folk they exert an immense pressure on behaviour. They are so powerful because in primitive groups, where face-to-face contacts prevail, no one can escape beyond the range of group opinion and group control. The authority of customs diminishes in complex society where impersonal relations largely replace personal contact and where individuals are further removed from the direct control of the group as a whole. But apart from the growth of society as such, there are other factors making for the disintegration of customs in modern society. Money economy disintegrates customs because they are too slow in their workings. In a society where production for the market and payment in money, not in kind, are dominant, legal rules expressly made for the situation and promptly enforceable are necessary. Any strong organisation of economic or military power works against custom. The reason is that customs tend to differ in different localities, whereas a strict organisation like the army needs homogeneous rules over all its spheres of action. Custom is obeyed more spontaneously because it grows slowly and can thus penetrate the whole web of human relationships, emotionally engaging all members of the group. Therefore as long as customs spontaneously prevail, they are the strongest ties in building up a social order and at this level they are equal to a moral order. The spontaneous conformity which results from them is an asset that should remain untouched as long as it prevails. In England the power of custom is greater than in any other industrial society, and here the laws have gradually developed out of the background of custom.

3. LAW AS A FORM OF SOCIAL CONTROL

Law is the code upheld by the State. It is a body of rules which is recognised, interpreted and applied to particular situations by the courts of the State. Whereas custom develops unconsciously, law is consciously created and put into force at the moment of its enactment. The transition from custom to law is just a part of the general rationalisation in modern society, a change which can be observed equally in all departments of life. Activities which were at one time performed unconsciously are now consciously formulated, their concepts defined and their principles set out. The former range of variation is reduced and hard and fast rules tend to prevail. This is one of the factors which makes a modern society a more exactly functioning machine, but on the other hand its vitality decreases. The disadvantage of law is also, as Sir Henry Maine pointed out, that it is only known by a privileged minority. According to him social necessities and social opinions are always in advance of law. Thus a continuous readjustment to changing conditions is necessary.

The functions of law vary to a certain extent in different societies. According to the philosophy of liberalism, law had two main tasks to fulfil, to maintain a fundamental order within which man should find security and opportunity and to adjust those conflicts and interests between individuals and groups which they cannot settle for themselves, or in the settling of which they encroach upon the interests of others.

Modern totalitarian methods would not be satisfied with such a definition because they are not usually satisfied with merely laying down the rules of the game, but aim at prescribing every action of individual play.

4. PRESTIGE AND LEADERSHIP

Social controls, custom and law, represent the objective aspect of authority. But authority is always exercised by individuals, and we speak of people with prestige and authority. There must be authority in every society, but the sources of authority may be different. It is wrong to identify authority with the application of brute force for authority based on force alone is exceptional and cannot be permanent. The sources and methods of exercising authority vary with time and with the structure of society. Among tradition-loving people authority is vested in certain families—the king, the hereditary nobility, the priesthood etc. Among peoples inclined to hero-worship authority is vested in the man of destiny—for instance in the hero of Homeric epics. Among religious people authority is vested in the intermediaries between the Divinity and man, for instance the hierarchy of the Church. Among war-like peoples it is vested in great warriors, in materialistic civilisation in business magnates, among democratic peoples in political leaders who claim to recreate the will of the people. In Russia, Marxism is worshipped as a scientific source of authority. The objection to this attitude is not that a society should not be built upon a scientific basis, but that it is contrary to the nature of science that any teaching should be taken as final truth. Many of the struggles in history are struggles between two types of authority—religious and political, democratic and totalitarian.

We must make a clear distinction between two basic types of authority. First, when authority is vested in office, and second when it is vested in a personal leader. An example of the first case is when we obey a policeman or other official; we do so not because of his personal qualities, but because he represents a social control, his authority is a borrowed authority. This kind of authority prevails in static societies and is strongest where there is least inclination for revolution or disorganisation. Authority based upon personal leadership is usually manifested in dynamic society when the leader is obeyed on account of his personal qualities. The prophets of Israel, Mahomet, Napoleon, Lenin, Hitler and Mussolini, are examples of personal leadership. Within the framework of analytic sociology the sociologist is deliberately unconcerned with the content of their doctrines and expresses no opinion as to the truth or falsity of their teaching, but interests himself primarily in the nature of their authority. In the contrast between the prophets and mystics on the one hand and the priesthood on the other, one can clearly see the two forms of authority at variance. The opportunity for the personal leader occurs when society is in a state of disorganisation and new norms of conduct must be found. The perturbed masses, seeking for new solutions, are prepared to accept the new valuations and patterns of conduct presented by the leader.

I agree with MacIver's definition of leadership as the power to direct men which is based on personal qualities and not on tenure of office. While authority bases its claims on facts and is respected for this reason, prestige may be gained by the mere appearance of power. Though this may be considered the accepted definition, Harold Nicolson draws attention to the fact that the word prestige means different things in England, France and Germany, and shows in a very illuminating way that the different interpretations of the word reflect different types of policy. He claims that it is the aim of traditional English policy to base power upon reputation rather than to base reputation upon power. To the French the word prestige has the connotation of glamour, romance, desire to deceive. To them prestige is not a political method but mainly an emotional effect. In German the nearest word to prestige may be translated as national honour. This term reflects a lack of self-confidence and is connected with the almost hysterical reaction which many Germans feel when their status in the world is in danger.

Mr. Nicolson then goes on to say that the traditional English attitude is that prestige cannot be acquired without power, yet it cannot be retained without reputation. The consequence of this attitude was that the English ruled gently and tried to avoid provocation but on the other hand tended to neglect defensive power whereby the offensive power of other nations has correspondingly increased. The value of Nicolson's analysis is that he shows that the different interpretations of the same words in different countries reflect the varying modes of action prevailing in these countries.

5. THE PHILOSOPHICAL AND SOCIOLOGICAL INTERPRETATION OF VALUES

In all the cases we have discussed, valuation has played a considerable part. Custom, law, leadership, prestige, represent phenomena in which valuation is inherent, though we do not yet know what valuations are nor how they come about and change. As we have seen, most of the struggles in history are due to the clash between two different forms of allegiance to authority, or to a change in valuations. What are values? To the idealist philosopher—even to the man in the street—they present themselves as eternal qualities, as gifts or commands from Heaven, as transcendental forces. To the sociologist they are part and parcel of the social process—functions of the social process. To him values are not abstract entities nor are they intrinsic qualities of an object. In the light of concrete analysis it is meaningless to speak of values as if they existed independent of the valuating subject or the group for which they are valid.

We have a deep resistance to this approach. It is rooted in our thought habits to imagine that we believe in values

131

because they are eternal, presented by some superhuman or super-historical power. Further, we are reluctant to change this attitude because we are afraid of the relativism which may follow the realisation that values are created by society and vary in different societies, and that our own values are also dependent on our social system. However, just as science had to break the thought habit that the sun went round the earth, although the acceptance of this fact seemed to endanger the religious and moral order of the time, so we must accept the fact that values are socially generated—if this is the case. But on consideration we will realise that our sense of obligation to these values need not diminish because we accept the fact that they are not dictated by some transcendental command but by our rational insight into the needs of our social order. What will really happen will be that the theological and philosophical obligation will be replaced by a sociological one. The theological and to a large extent the philosophical justification of values appeals to the thought habits of men accustomed to act under authority, whilst the sociological approach appeals to the democratically educated man because the social obligation can be reasonably tested. Another advantage of the sociological concept is that it both explains the obligation and opens the door to reforms, whereas the old absolute conception rendered reform slower.

Let us take a very simple concrete situation in which valuation occurs. I wish to drive a nail into a piece of wood and I therefore look at everything in terms of its 'hammer value'—that is to say, measure its capacity to meet the special situation. I try out different objects; some of them are effective and become active factors in the context of my life. In this case, as in other cases, there is no abstract value, but certain things become valuable in the context of a certain activity, through performing a desired function. As a matter of fact the 'hammer value' corresponds to an emotionalisation of certain functions which become important in our lives. That is to say, the value is not inherent in any object or activity as such, but each may become valuable if it becomes necessary and therefore emphasised in the context of life. For instance, if through a war situation ambulance driving becomes an important occupation, all the activities connected with it will become emotionalised and valuable. If in the context of life it is important that I should learn shorthand, anything connected with this becomes emotionalised and valuable. In any value-generating situation therefore there are three factors: an organism, a situation and an object.

The organism is necessary to give meaning to the idea of value. It is not necessary to be conscious of the values that motivate us. The situation is the immediate occasion for action, in view of which the organism meets the situation, by an act of selection which is a step in its growth. According to Cooley, one can distinguish two kinds of values, human nature values and institutional values. To the first belong those which like the taste for salt and the pleasure in bright colours are fairly general in mankind. These human nature values are very few in number because most of our value attitudes are bred by institutions. For instance the values of the Roman Catholic Church, the values of the English, the values of the Nazi system, the values of a professional organisation or of an army. Institutional values are much greater in number and can only be studied with reference to their social antecedents —that is to say their history and the whole situation of the group. Because of this organic character, values vary with the time, the group and the social class. Within the frame of these group values each individual may have a value system of his own which is a variation of the institutional values within his reach. The individual approach to the problem of values leads us to believe that we ourselves are the original sources of our value systems. This is true to a certain extent—without the spontaneity of the individual no further development or value creation would be possible. But it is a delusion to think that the value system which we obey can be explained in terms of our personal life history. Most of the values which dominate our lives are linked up as we have seen with the institutions and groups in which we live, and very many changes in valuations can be traced back to the historical changes in the group and to changing functional needs. For example, H. M. Chadwick in his book *The Heroic Age* has shown how in a very short time during the great migration of the peoples, an opportunity was given to adventurous groups for easy conquest. This produced a division between the warrior groups and the peasant community in the Germanic tribes, to which the creation of a completely different scale of values corresponded. In the peasant community the former values of the community, conformity, mutual help, valuation of labour, were maintained. In the new warrior group the values of an heroic gang suddenly developed, individualism, bravery, readiness to pillage, personal allegiance to a leader; these values are, as it were, counter values. Whereas in the original group conformity and mutual help were virtues, here individualism and pillage prevail. The two sets of values are reflected in the gods worshipped by the Germanic tribes. The tribal ethics of the community are represented by Thor, an old peasant, and Wotan is the warrior god. As we see, society organised for labour produced a different set of values from that produced by a society organised for conflict.

To return to our original example, the warrior society tried to establish the new authority of a personal leader as against the established authority of the elders in the tribe. A kind of propaganda vaunting their new values in preference to the old community values was necessary. The new leaders with their small courts and retinues were a kind of *parvenu* power which needed justification and advertisement. This responsibility was given to the *scop*—

the poet. When we look at this poetry to-day, we see that it had two aims, first to establish the prestige and authority of the hero, who was present at its recital, and second to inculcate the values and patterns of life necessary to warrior society. Thus we see that in the making of new values an organic growth is at work. But the valuation is carried out by certain functionaries—as for instance the prestige lender, in this case the poet, who disseminates the value. The same basic situation can also be observed in the Renaissance where we have the rise of a new class out of traditional medieval society, the class of efficient bankers, industrialists and merchants who in contrast to the conventional values of the medieval community laid emphasis upon personality, extravagance, heroism, art. In this case it is again the poet and the artist who were the prestige lenders. Of course this does not mean that art and poetry are only a kind of advertisement, but we must realise two things. First that the sociologist must clearly understand that art and poetry did in fact have this function among others, and that prestige lenders have always existed; second that though the technique of advertisement has only lately been developed in detail, it has always existed in some form.

CHAPTER XII

Causes of Social Change

After having analysed the factors of social stability, we have to answer the question: what are the primary causes which make society dynamic, thus compelling both the groups and the individuals to re-make their adjustments continually? As the Marxist theory of social change is the most consistent, and very widely discussed, it will prove useful to take it as a starting point for our discussion of the causes of social change.

1. THE MARXIST THEORY OF SOCIAL CHANGE

The Marxist theory of social change is the reflection of an age which witnessed the industrial revolution and realised the great significance of the change in economic technique. For this reason this theory is on the one hand highly sensitive to the technical factor, and on the other is apt to over-emphasise it. The right approach to this theory is to take it as a challenge.

The ultimate cause of social change according to the theory is 'the material forces of production'. These forces, as represented by economic technique, are subject to change, new inventions occur and these alter not only the machinery but the primary socio-economic relationships. By the latter is understood those human relationships which are directly determined by the changing division of labour which goes with the changed technique. Primary relations are the *paterfamilias* and his slave,

136

the craftsman and his apprentice, the entrepreneur and the wage-earning labourer. Primary socio-economic relationships connected to a society depending upon the hand mill, are other than those which are necessary to a society based upon steam and electricity. In Marx's words 'the sum total of these relations of production constitutes the economic structure of society, the real foundation on which rise legal and political superstructures, and to which correspond definite forms of social consciousness'. In this famous statement the idea is established that the basic organisation of society is expressed in its economic structure which to a large extent determines the legal and political organisations, and even the form of social consciousness; that is to say, the kind of thought and ideas people hold in any particular age. Whether one accepts this statement or not, its value consists in its hint that there is a correlation between the economic structure of a society and its legal and political organisation, and that even the world of our thought is affected by these relationships. One can interpret Marx's statement in a deterministic sense, as if the superstructure were definitely shaped by the basic structure. This is obviously going too far, but it is important to realise this point of view as a scientific hypothesis which induces us to study the legal and political setting of a society and its world of thought in a continuous relationship with the economic and social changes. It cannot be denied for instance that the legal organisation—the property system for instance—varies with the changing economic structure, or that the political and other ideas people hold are somehow connected with the social context in which they live.

How exactly does social change, according to this theory, come about and spread throughout the different spheres of society? Firstly, as we have seen, the material forces of production are subject to change through technical inventions, and thus a rift arises between the economic factors and the socio-economic relationships built upon them. The whole superstructure must change. For instance, our whole legal organisation, with its property system, was largely adjusted to meet the needs of a stage of industrialisation in which small economic units carried on production. To-day, as a consequence of inventions, large-scale industrial techniques dominate and the concentration of capital or state ownership should correspond to this. But this change does not come about easily, for the older order has created vested interests and ideologies which resist any alteration. Therefore the new forces of production are, as it were, fettered, and this leads to a strong tension and eventually to revolutionary outbursts. Who can break this spell of ideologies, of wrong habits of thought and vested interest? Only those who are, as it were, excluded from this order and are able to awaken to the consciousness of its decay. This is the proletariat, which is not interested in the maintenance of a superstructure which prevents the changed economic conditions from creating the social conditions under which it could work smoothly. So the Marxist theory runs and I now wish to make some critical comment.

In my view it is a useful approach to the problem to start with an analysis of society by focusing attention first on the technical foundations of its economic production. This is a sphere where change can be clearly observed and defined. Here I think one should go even further than Marx. He was only concerned with the changes in the techniques of economic production, the visible machinery which produces food, clothes, housing, and so on. But these are not the only techniques in which change influences society—for instance there are improvements in military technique which influence the shape of society equally. We have the opportunity of seeing that changes in military technique have made the domination of the army and of armed gangs more likely. In the same way we can see that the improvement of what I would call social techniques influences the course of events. For instance, modern methods of influencing human behaviour made propaganda a powerful agent, and those who have a grip on it may seek to influence society in any direction they please. In the same way improvement in the technique of organisation has brought about the power of bureaucracy, and it is a new managerial bureaucracy which is competing with the competitive class of captains of industry. All this shows that not only changed economic techniques influence the primary socio-economic relationships, and through them the whole of society, but improvements in the fields of other techniques supplement this influence. Whilst it is true that technological change influences what happens in societies, is there no scope for exercising the power of the mind in social affairs?

Some people think the mind is impotent to influence social affairs, others that it is omnipotent. Whilst I believe that technological factors are important, I should maintain that they may be manoeuvred according to human ends which are culturally agreed. Or, as Lewis Mumford puts it, 'our capacity to go beyond the machine rests in our power to assimilate the machine'. In our advanced technical age it would be impossible to destroy the machine but it is possible with intelligence to remove those institutions which do harm, or strengthen those tendencies which are already at work and useful but not yet fully developed. Social reform does not mean building society anew from the beginning, but observing the tendencies at work and through a definite strategy guiding it in the desired direction.

2. CLASS AND CASTE CONFLICT AS CAUSES OF SOCIAL CHANGE

Both class and caste refer to social position which means only that certain people have different chances in life according to the place they take in the social order. Caste or estate is a more rigid form of defining one's status in society and is based upon religious or legal regulations (taboos, laws, customs) limiting the scope of rise or fall in the social scale. Class is a more elastic definition of one's place in the social order. There are, in the main, no legal barriers, but only those of an economic and educational nature which make it difficult for certain classes to rise in the social scale. Modern society in the age of liberalism and democracy has transformed the system of estates into that of open classes. In medieval society, the society of estates, you were generally confined all your life to the social estate in which you were born. Modern capitalist society does not recognise such legal limitations but economic and educational handicaps may prove difficult to surmount. Although in everyday talk we think we are quite clear as to the meaning of class distinction, the more closely one examines its actual content the vaguer its form becomes. In considering the different definitions it may be useful to discriminate between the descriptive and the functional definition of class.

The descriptive definition of class is only concerned with the question of the distinguishing marks classifying people into classes. This definition does not attempt to give a deeper explanation of the dynamic causes bringing about class differentiation in connection with the changing social structure. This is the concern of the functional definition. Ginsberg attempted such a descriptive definition and found that in practice the basis of distinction into classes varies. We classify a person as lower class, middle class or upper class, according to his behaviour, speech, dress, habits of social intercourse, but we consider as more important distinguishing marks, economic status, which is defined by property and income, occupation, education, mode of life. All this means that our discriminating sense operates with a combination of points of view but these points of view vary in predominance. It is interesting that this distinction between higher and lower seems to develop in every social order whereas it cannot be made a general rule that either property or education or occupation or mode of life, are the main distinguishing marks in a given society.

The functional definition differs from the descriptive in that it groups those people together who have the same function in society, and therefore are expected to act in the same way and to develop a similar consciousness. Marx tries to define the position in society in terms of economic functions, and he therefore speaks of economic classes. According to this theory, persons who hold the same position in the process of production belong together, and so you have on the one hand the owners of the means of production and on the other the producing classes. As the forms of production affect the forms of distribution, a social class is also characterised by the source of income. Taking these two things together one arrives at the definition that a social class is an aggregate of persons who have the same functions in the productive process and who therefore have the same source of income.

The picture would be too simple if we were to distinguish only two classes, the owners of the means of production and the non-owners. Marx was aware of the fact that in addition to the basic classes there are found in every society intermediate classes, occupying a middle position between the commanding and the executing classes. There are for instance the transitional classes, resulting from the disintegration of the previous forms of industrial production—such as the small entrepreneurs and tradesmen. There are also the mixed classes, such as the corporate bureaucracy, the white collared workers, the professionals, the great army of the new distributive occupations, such as the employees of the big department stores, and the *déclassé* groups consisting of beggars, vagrants and the like. This functional definition enabled Marx to link up his theory of social change with the class structure of society. The classes play a certain role in the transformation of society, the original cause of which, according to Marx, is to be found in the changing economic technique. The dynamic process comes about in this way: those who carry out the physical work produce surplus profit—a certain amount of goods above their own consumption. Then there is a struggle for the distribution of the total national product and as this struggle becomes conscious it gives rise to class interests and class conflicts. Gradually class interests develop into a system which embraces all life and these interests are interwoven with political, religious and scientific interests, the result of which is the gradual development of class ideals and a definite class psychology. Each class tends to develop a frame of mind, a *Weltanschauung*.

The existence of class interests does not mean that they are always understood by a class itself. You may belong to a class, according to Marx, because you are a wage-earner, but if you are a white-collared worker, you are likely to conceal from yourself the fact that you are a wage-earner and share the interests and prejudices of the capitalist class. In this case, claims Marx, you have a 'false consciousness' and it is only through enlightenment and propaganda that you will understand your real position in society. It is difficult to show clearly the existence of class consciousness. For instance, a ruling class might try to diminish the awareness of class positions, or it may be that among members of a class temporary interests clash with general or long-range interests. According to Marx, class consciousness in the suppressed classes can be concealed for a long time, but sooner or later the antagonisms existing in the social order are bound to lead to a social revolution: 'Sooner or later when the productive forces of society reach a point when their further development is obstructed by existing social institutions, the class struggle becomes acute and it is then that it becomes the main driving force of social reorganisation.' In that revolution the proletariat has to capture the state and its whole machinery in order to remove those obsolete institutions which prevent the development of the productive forces and maintain the class structure.

3. CRITICISM OF THE MARXIST THEORY OF CLASS STRUGGLE. THE ROLE OF RELIGIOUS AND NATIONAL DIFFERENCES

Before putting forward my criticism of Marx's theory, I wish to emphasise its value even although in many ways it may be misleading. Its main virtue is that it tries to look at society as a coherent structure, as a mechanism, the rules of which, if they are found, can be consistently interpreted. This means that Marx replaces the piece-meal interpretation by a coherent hypothesis which helps us to reconstruct the working of the whole with the aid of imagination. In the natural sciences, if the variety and changes of factors are too great, we try to construct a model which reduces the variety to a simplified scheme in order to get away from the confusion and despondency. Without such a hypothetical simplification, the human mind could not grasp the whole. If we take the Marxian analysis of social change and class struggle as such a model and hypothesis, but not as a dogmatic statement of reality, then it will serve a useful purpose, all the more as we have no other coherent hypothesis and model of the structure of society. The physicist in trying to offer an interpretation of data will develop a model or a hypothesis. By this he will not mean that reality is bound to conform to his model, but he will only claim that his model approximates to what happens in reality. But if the variations in the data become too great for the hypothesis to explain, he will have to be ready to replace it by another model which takes into account the great number of changes which do not fit into the original theory. The trouble about the Marxists is that they do not take the Marxian hypothesis as a hypothesis, but as a dogmatic statement from which one is not allowed to deviate. This distorts the value of the whole approach. These preliminary remarks will help to show where the picture of reality deviates from the Marxist model.

For logical purposes it was quite useful to aim at a functional definition which artificially classifies society into two classes; the class of the owners of the means of production and the producing class. But if we look at reality and ask ourselves whether the people really act and behave according to these distinctions, we can only assert that there is a *tendency* towards the formation of economic and social groups and their stratification and stability vary from one society to another in accordance with general economic conditions. In a marginal situation it may be that people will act against each other according to this antagonism, but in most situations the dividing principle does not rise to the surface. The many other aspects enumerated in the descriptive definition of classes are continually at work modifying the functional division.

Marx originally saw the middle class as crushed between the millstones of the capitalist and the workers, and as a dwindling group. Actually the elaboration of capitalism has made it a growing group. He was right about the dwindling of the small entrepreneur and tradesman, but meanwhile a new middle class has developed. This class consists of technicians, white-collared groups, professional groups, those engaged in the marketing and distributive system, small business men, small investors, the housewives, the people with annuities and small founded incomes. A social theory which does not reckon with their special dynamics will be misleading. One of the reasons for the rise of Fascism is that the Italian and German working class parties alienated these groups by not realising their special psychology and lacking a constructive scheme which would have provided them with an active function in their movement.

In the same way, the statement that class struggles are inevitable is an unjustified generalisation, for it is only a tendency and not the only form of transformation of societies. There is no doubt that in modern society there is a latent struggle between economic and social groups, but this struggle is fragmentary and intermittent; often it may become completely latent, although it cannot be denied that if no other outlet is given to reform it may become the dominant feature.

If one takes it as a tendency, there will only be struggle if through reform we are unable to remove those institutions which hamper the evolution of the modern economic system, and thus cause continuous crises in it. But on principle revolution can always be avoided if these transformations are carried out gradually and in a peaceful way. If from the very beginning we state that the struggle is, and must be, inevitable, we sap reform. On the other hand, one has of course always to be alive to the possibility that through frustration revolution may become unavoidable.

Moreover, the formation of consciousness of the general interest of the class is slow and intermittent. It is inevitable that economic groups which are closely related should sometimes struggle against one another as well as against opposing groups. It is also inevitable that economic interests should be overshadowed from time to time by cultural, religious and ethnic factors. Nationalism both as an economic and as a cultural phenomenon, tends to offset the formation of classes. It would be more correct to say that the tendency to unite along the lines of class interests is one of the great tendencies in our modern societies, with which the tendency to unite along cultural, religious or national lines competes. The Second World War, for instance, is an example of class interests being over-ridden by national interests. The direction in which integration takes place very often depends on the situation, on where the challenge comes from. A Socialist

Catholic German miner in the Ruhr district, for instance, will react in terms of his *national* feelings if attack comes from an enemy to his country. The same man might be dominated by his *religious* traditions and emotions when he finds his Catholicism attacked. Finally, in a struggle in which he feels that his class allegiance is in jeopardy, his *socialist* feelings are uppermost. This approach prevents us from dealing with people as if they were to be put into separate drawers labelled 'Socialist', 'German', etc., for such classifications do not correspond to the dynamic nature of human motivations. Everybody is guided by a set of various motivations, and it depends, as we have seen, on the situation which comes to the fore.

With this more elastic theory, we are able to understand that this age is equally the scene of increased nationalism and increased class struggle, and it depends on the historical situation and the management of these situations, which tendencies will integrate. As an exclusive generalisation it is not true to say either that our age is one of class struggles or one of national differences. At the same time, the history of Europe from 1930 to 1945 has shown that, temporarily at least, class divisions can be over-ridden by the mobilisation of nationalist feelings. If we take the class struggle, not as a dogmatic necessity, but as a tendency, we are better able to understand the great structural changes in our society. We have to have both a comprehensive hypothesis and, at the same time, an elastic way of thinking which is always ready to adapt the hypothesis to the new realities.

Bibliography[1]

PART 1

CHAPTER I: MAN AND HIS PSYCHIC EQUIPMENT

1. *Behaviour, Situation and Adjustment*

Davis, J., and Barnes, H. E., et al.: *Introduction to Sociology.* Boston, 1927.
(Especially Book II, Part III.)

Folsom, J. K.: *Culture and the Social Process.* New York, 1928.
(Especially Chapter IV.)

Healey, H., et al.: *Reconstructing Behaviour in Youth.* New York, 1929.

Parmelee, M.: *The Science of Human Behaviour.* New York, 1913.

Paton, S.: *Human Behaviour.* New York, 1921.

Sapir, E.: 'The Unconscious Patterning of Behaviour in Society'.
(See Child, C. M., Koffka, K., et al.: *The Unconscious: A Symposium.* New York, 1928.)

Thomas, W. I.: 'The Behaviour Patterns and the Situation'.
(See Burgess, E. W. (Ed.): *Personality and the Group.* Chicago, 1929.)

Zilsel, E.: 'Geschichte und Biologie, Überlieferung und Vererbung', *Archiv. f. Socialwissenschaft*, Vol. 65, 1931.

[1] In compiling the bibliography we have selected from the many titles gathered together in Mannheim's notes those which seemed to us especially relevant to his argument. As can be seen in some of his other books, Mannheim built up very large lists of titles in his bibliographies, and we thought that we should prefer to be selective. We have followed the principle of listing the titles in the same way as he did according to the chapter and subdivision headings to be found in the table of contents.

J. E.
W. A. C. S.

2. i. *Habits and the Problem of 'Instincts'*

Dewey, J.: *Human Nature and Conduct*. New York, 1930.

Douglas, A. T.: 'Habits, Their Formation, Their Value, Their Danger', *Mental Hygiene*, Vol. 16, 1932.

Ellwood, C. H.: 'Mental Patterns in Social Evolution', *Publications of the American Sociological Society*, 1922.

James, W.: *Principles of Psychology*. New York, 1890.

McDougall, W.: *An Introduction to Social Psychology*. Boston, 1921.

McDougall, W.: *Energies of Men*. New York, 1933.

McDougall, W.: 'Organization of the Affective Life', *Acta Psychologica*, Vol. 2, 1937.

Mead, G. H.: 'Scientific Method and Social Sciences', *Journal of Ethics*, Vol. 29.

Murphy, G., Murphy, L. B., and Newcomb, T. M.: *Experimental Social Psychology*. New York, 1937. (Especially Chapter III.)

Park, E., and Burgess, E. W.: *Introduction to the Science of Sociology*. Chicago, 1928. (Especially Chapters IX, X and XI.)

Thouless, R. H.: *General and Social Psychology*. London, 1937.

Williams, G. M.: *Our Rural Heritage*. New York, 1925.

Znaniecki, F.: *The Laws of Social Psychology*. Chicago, 1925.

ii. *The Habit-making Mechanism*

Bernard, L. L.: *An Introduction to Social Psychology*. New York, 1926.

Bernard, L. L.: 'Neuro-Psychic Technique in Social Evolution', *Publications of the American Sociological Society*, Vol. 18, Chicago, 1924.

Davis, M. M.: *Psychological Interpretations of Society*. New York, 1929.

Douglas, A. T.: 'Habits, Their Formation, Their Value, Their Danger', *Mental Hygiene*, Vol. 16, 1932.

Jennings, H. S., Watson, J. B., Meyer, A., and Thomas, W. I.: *Suggestions of Modern Science Concerning Education*. New York, 1918.

Pavlov, I.: *Lectures on Conditioned Reflexes*. New York, 1928.

Tarde, G.: *The Laws of Imitation* (translated by E. C. Parsons). New York, 1903.

Watson, J. B.: *The Ways of Behaviourism*. New York, 1928.

Watson, J. B.: *Behaviourism*. London, 1931.

Watson, J. B., and McDougall, E.: *The Battle of Behaviourism*. Psyche Miniatures, General Series, No. 19.

3. *Evolution in the Models of Imitation*

Burgess, E. W., et al.: *Environment and Education*. Chicago, 1942.

Burgess, E. W.: 'The Cultural Approach to the Study of Personality', *Mental Hygiene*, Vol. 14, 1930.

Burgess, E. W.: *Personality and the Social Group*. Chicago, 1929.

Burrow, T.: 'Alternating Frames of Reference in the Sphere of Human Behaviour', *Journal of Social Philosophy*, Vol. 2, No. 2.

Cooley, C. H.: *Human Nature and the Social Order*. New York, 1928.

(Especially Chapter XIII.)

Groves, E. R.: *Personality and Social Adjustment*. New York, 1931.

Smith, W. R.: 'Social Education in the School through Group Activities', *Publications of the American Sociological Society*, Vol. 13, 1922.

Smith, W. R.: *Principles of Educational Sociology*. Boston, 1929.

Thrasher, F. N.: *The Gang*. Chicago, 1927.

4. *Sociological and Psychoanalytic Descriptions of Man*
    i. *Repression ii. Neurosis, Reaction Formation and Projection*
    iii. *Rationalisation*

Alexander, A.: *The Psychoanalysis of the Total Personality* (translated by B. Glück and B. Lewin). New York, 1930.

Allport, G. W.: *Personality. A Psychological Interpretation*. New York, 1937.

Bain, R.: 'Sociology and Psychoanalysis', *American Sociological Review*, Vol. 1, No. 2, 1936.

Burgess, E. W.: 'Freud and Sociology in the United States', *American Journal of Sociology*, Vol. 45, 1939–40.

Dashiell, J. F.: *Fundamentals of General Psychology*. Boston, 1937.

Dashiell, J. F.: 'Experimental Studies on the Influence of Social Situations upon the Behaviour of Individual Human Adults'.
(See Murchison, C. (Ed.): *A Handbook of Social Psychology*. Worcester, Mass., 1935.)

Folsom, J. K.: *Social Psychology*. New York, 1931.
(Especially Chapters II and III.)

Folsom, J. K.: *The Family*. London, 1944.

Freud, A.: *The Ego and the Mechanism of Defence*. London, 1937.

Freud, S.: *A General Introduction to Psychoanalysis* (translated by G. S. Hall). New York, 1922.

Freud, S.: *Basic Writings* (translated by A. A. Brill). New York, 1938.

Healy, W., Bronner, A., and Bowers, A. M.: *The Structure and Meaning of Psychoanalysis*. New York, 1931.

Healy, W.: *Personality in Formation and Action*. London, 1938.

Jones, E.: *Papers on Psychoanalysis*. London, 1923.

Jones, E.: *Social Aspects of Psychoanalysis*. Lectures delivered under the auspices of the Sociological Society, London, 1924.

Jones, E.: 'Abnormal Psychology and Social Psychology'.
(See MacFie Campbell, C., McDougall, W., et al.: *Problems of Personality. Studies presented to Morton Prince*. London, 1932.)

Lasswell, H. D.: *Psychopathology and Politics*. Chicago, 1930.

Schilder, P.: 'Psychoanalysis and Conditioned Reflexes', *The Psychoanalytic Review*, Vol. 29, No. 1, 1937.

Taylor, W. S.: 'Rationalization and its Social Significance', *Journal of Abnormal and Social Psychology*, Vol. 18, 1923.

iv. *Symbolisation and Daydreaming*

Blumer, M.: *Movies and Conduct*. New York, 1933.

Healy, W., et al.: *op. cit.*

Jones, E.: 'The Theory of Symbolism', *Papers on Psychoanalysis*. London, 1923.

Sachs, H.: *The Creative Unconscious*. Cambridge, Mass., 1951.
Schilder, P.: 'The Analysis of Ideologies as a Psychotherapeutic Method', *American Journal of Psychiatry*, Vol. 93, 1936.

v. *Sublimation and Idealisation and their Social Significance*

Bartlett, F. C.: 'The Psychological Process of Sublimation', *Scientia*, Vol. 43, 1928.
Dashiell, J. F.: 'The "Inner" Life as Suppressed Ideal of Conduct', *International Journal of Ethics*, Vol. 30, 1919–20.
Durkheim, E.: *Le Suicide*. Paris, 1897 (English translation, London, 1952).
Jones, E.: 'The Significance of Sublimation Processes for Education and Re-education', *Papers on Psychoanalysis*. London, 1923.
Lasswell, H. D.: 'The Triple Appeal Principle. A Contribution of Psychoanalysis to Political and Social Science', *American Journal of Sociology*, Vol. 37, 1931–32.
Lasswell, H. D.: 'What Psychiatrists and Political Scientists can learn from one another', *Psychiatry*, Vol. 1, 1938.
Mead, G. H.: *Mind, Self, and Society*. Chicago, 1934.
Pepper, S. C.: 'The Boundaries of Society', *International Journal of Ethics*, Vol. 32, 1921–22.
Taylor, W. S.: 'Alternative Response as a Form of Sublimation', *Psychological Review*, 1932.
Weber, Max: *Essays in Sociology From Max Weber* (translated and edited by H. H. Gerth and C. W. Mills). London, New York, 1947.
Znaniecki, F.: *The Laws of Social Psychology*. Chicago, 1925.

CHAPTER II: MAN AND HIS PSYCHIC EQUIPMENT (*Continued*)

5. *The Social Guidance of Psychic Energies*
Allport, F. H.: *Institutional Behaviour*. Chapell Hill, North Carolina, 1933.
Bernard, L. L.: *Social Control*. New York, 1937.
Dewey, J.: 'Social Science and Social Control', *New Republic*, Vol. 18, 1931.

Hart, H.: 'The Transmutation of Motivation', *American Journal of Sociology*, Vol. 35, 1929–30.

Jones, A. J.: *Principles of Guidance*. London, New York, 1934.

Mannheim, Karl: *Man and Society in an Age of Reconstruction*. London, 1940.

Merriam, C. E.: *The Making of Citizens: a Comparative Study of the Methods of Civic Training*. Chicago, 1931.

Osborn, R.: *Freud and Marx*. London, 1937.

Overstreet, H. A.: *Influencing Human Behaviour*. London, 1926.

6. *Object Fixation and the Transference of Libido*

Allport, G. W.: 'Attitudes'.
(See Murchison, C. (Ed.): *A Handbook of Social Psychology*. Worcester, Mass., 1935.)

Burrow, T.: *The Biology of Human Conflict. An Anatomy of Human Behaviour, Individual and Social*. New York, 1937.

Burrow, T.: 'Altering Frames of Reference in the Sphere of Human Behaviour', *Journal of Social Psychology*, Vol. 2, 1937.

Faris, E.: 'Attitudes and Behaviour', *American Journal of Sociology*, Vol. 34, 1928–29.

Faris, E.: 'The Concept of Social Attitudes', *Journal of Applied Sociology*, Vol. 9, 1925.

Folsom, J. K.: *The Family: its Sociology and Social Psychiatry*, 1934.

Frank, L. K.: 'Physiological Tension and Social Structure', *Publications of the American Sociological Society*, Vol. 22, 1928.

French, T. M.: *Social Conflict and Psychic Conflict*. Chicago, 1939.

Freud, S.: *Reflections* (translated by A. A. Brill and B. Kuttner). New York, 1922.

Jones, A. J.: *Principles of Guidance*. New York, London, 1934.

Lasswell, H. D.: *Psychopathology and Politics*. Chicago, 1931.

Mead, M.: 'Adolescence in Primitive and Modern Society'.
(See Calverton, V. F., and Schmalhausen, S. D. (Eds.): *The New Generation*. London and New York, 1930.)

BIBLIOGRAPHY

Park, R.: 'Human Nature, Attitudes and the Mores'.
(See Young, K. (Ed.): *Social Attitudes*. New York, 1931.)
Reuter, E. B., Mead, M., and Foster, R. G.: 'Sociological Research in Adolescence', *American Journal of Sociology*, Vol. 42, 1936–37.
Wallas, G.: *Our Social Heritage*. London, 1921.
Waelder, R.: 'Aetiologie und Verlauf der Massenpsychose', *Imago*, Vol. 21, 1935.

7. *Sociology of Types of Behaviour*
  i. *Attitudes and Wishes*
    Allport, G. W., and Schanck, R. L.: 'Are Attitudes Biological or Cultural in Origin?', *Character and Personality*, 1936.
    Allport, G. W.: *Personality. A Psychological Interpretation*. New York, 1937.
    Folsom, J. K.: *Social Psychology*. London and New York, 1931.
    Frank, J. O.: 'Some Psychological Determinants of the Level of Aspiration', *American Journal of Psychology*, Vol. 47, 1935.
    Thomas, W. I., and Znaniecki, F.: *The Polish Peasant in Europe and America*. New York, 1927.
    Thomas, W. I.: *The Unadjusted Girl*. Boston, 1928.
    Thomas, W. I.: 'The Persistence of Primary-Group Norms in Present-day Society'.
    (See Jennings, H. S., Watson, J. B., et al.: *Suggestions of Modern Science Concerning Education*. New York, 1917.)
    Thorndike, E. L.: *The Psychology of Wants, Interests and Attitudes*. London and New York, 1935.
    Thorndike, E. L.: *Human Nature and the Social Order*. New York, 1940.

  ii. *Interests*
    Beaglehole, E.: *Property: a Study in Social Psychology*. London, 1931.
    MacIver, R. M.: *Society. A Textbook of Sociology*. New York, 1937.
    (Especially Chapter II.)
    Malinowski, B.: *Coral Gardens and their Magic*. New York, 1935.

153

Wallas, G.: *The Great Society. A Psychological Analysis.* London and New York, 1920.

Wright, H. W.: 'Rational Self-Interest and Social Adjustment', *International Journal of Ethics*, Vol. 30, 1919–20.

PART 2

THE MOST ELEMENTARY SOCIAL PROCESSES

CHAPTER III: A. SOCIAL CONTACT AND SOCIAL DISTANCE

1. *Primary and Secondary Contacts*

Burgess, E. W. (Ed.): 'The Urban Community', *Proceedings of the American Sociological Society*, Vol. 20, 1925.

Cooley, C. H.: *Social Organisation. A Study of the Larger Mind.* New York, 1924.

Ellwood, C. A.: *The Psychology of Human Society.* New York, 1925.

Kolb, J. H.: *Rural Primary Groups.* 1921.

Kolb, J. H., and Brunner, E.: *A Study of Rural Society.* Boston, 1935.

Park, R. E., and Burgess, E. W.: *Introduction to the Science of Sociology.* Chicago, 1928.
(Especially Chapter V.)

Simmel, G.: *Soziologie.* Leipzig, 1908.
(Especially Chapters 6, 9 and 10.)

Sorokin, P. A., and Zimmerman, C.: *Principles of Rural-Urban Sociology.* New York, 1929.

2. *Sympathetic and Categoric Contacts*

Eubank, E.: 'Errors of Sociology', *Social Forces.* 1937.

Lasswell, H. D.: *World Politics and Personal Insecurity.* New York, 1935.

Shaler, N. S.: *The Neighbour.* Boston, 1904.

Sumner, W. G.: *Folkways.* Boston, 1907.

Sperling, O.: 'Appersonierung und Excentrierung', *Internat. Zeitschrift f. Psychoanalyse*, Vol. 23, 1937.

Pilgrim Trust: *Men Without Work.* A Report. Cambridge, 1938.

3. *Social Distance*

Bogardus, E. S.: 'Measuring Social Distance', *Journal of Applied Sociology*, Vol. 9, 1925.

Bogardus, E. S.: 'Social Distance and its Implications', *ibid.*, Vol. 22, 1938.

Bogardus, E. S.: 'A Social Distance Scale', *Sociology and Social Research*, Vol. 17, 1932–33.

Bullough, E.: 'Psychological Distance as a Factor and an Aesthetic Principle', *British Journal of Psychology*, Vol. 5, 1912–13.

Park, R. E.: 'The Concept of Social Distance', *Journal of Applied Sociology*, Vol. 8, No. 6, 1924.

Révész, G.: 'Sozialpsychologische Betrachtungen an Affen', *Zeitschrift für Psychologie*, Vol. 118, 1930.

Schjelderup Ebbe, T.: 'Beiträge zur Sozialpsychologie des Haushuhns', *ibid.*, Vol. 88, 1922.

Schjelderup Ebbe, T.: 'Weitere Beiträge zur Sozial und Individualpsychologie des Haushuhns', *ibid.*, Vol. 92, 1923.

Sorokin, P.: *Social Mobility*. New York, 1927.

Wiese, L. v., and Becker, H.: *Systematic Sociology*. New York, 1932.

4. *Maintaining Social Hierarchy*

Pigors, P.: *Leadership or Domination*. London, 1936.

Raymond, E., and Kahn, E. E.: *The Craving for Superiority*. New Haven, 1931.

Simmel, G.: *Soziologie*. Leipzig, 1908. (Especially Chapter 3.)

Thomas, W. I.: *Primitive Behaviour*. New York, 1937.

CHAPTER IV: B. ISOLATION

1. *The Social Functions of Isolation*

Park R. E., and Burgess, E. W.: *Introduction to the Science of Sociology*. (Especially Chapter IV.)

Stock, W.: 'Isoliertheit und Verbundenheit', *Kölner Viertei-jahrshefte für Soziologie*, Jg. 2, 1922.

Yarros, V. S.: 'Isolation and Social Conflict', *American Journal of Sociology*, Vol. 27, 1921–22.

2. *The Various Kinds of Social Isolation*

Fromm, E.: 'Die gesellschaftlich Bedingtheit der psycho-analytischen Therapie', *Zeitschrift für Sozialforschung*, Jg. IV, 1935.

Geiger, T.: 'Formen der Vereinsamung', *Kölner Vierteljahrshefte für Soziologie*, Jg. 10, 1919.

Ichheiser, G.: 'Die Vereinsamung des Individuums', *Archiv f. Angewandte Psychologie*. Bd. 3.

Park R. E.: 'Human Migration and the Marginal Man', *American Journal of Sociology*, Vol. 33, 1927–28.

Sorokin, P. A.: *Social Mobility*. London, New York, 1927.

Stonequist, E. V.: *The Marginal Man*. New York, 1937.

Wood, M. M.: *The Stranger. A Study in Social Relationship*.

Wirth, L.: *The Ghetto*. Chicago, 1929.

CHAPTER V: INDIVIDUALISATION AND SOCIALISATION

C. Individualisation

Allport, F. H.: 'Self-evaluation: a Problem in Personal Development', *Mental Hygiene*. New York, 1925.

Benn, G.: *Der Neue Staat und die Intellectuellen*. Stuttgart, 1933.

Burgess, E. W.: *Personality and the Social Group*. Chicago, 1929.

Flugel, J. C.: *The Psychology of Clothes*. London, 1931.

Folsom, J. K.: *The Family: its Sociology and Social Psychiatry*. New York, 1934.

Horney, K.: 'The Problem of the Monogamous Ideal', *International Journal of Psychoanalysis*, Vol. 9, 1928.

Lewis, E. H.: 'Some Definitions of Individualization', *American Journal of Sociology*, Vol. 18, 1912–13.

Martin, A. H.: 'An Empirical Study of the Factors and Types of Voluntary Choice', *Archives of Psychology*, Vol. 51, 1922.

Mead, G. H.: 'The Genesis of the Self and Social Control', *International Journal of Ethics*, Vol. 35, 1925.

Mead, M.: *Coming of Age in Samoa*. New York, 1928.

Mead, M.: *Growing Up in New Guinea*. New York, 1930.

Misch, G.: *History of Autobiography in Antiquity*, Vol. 1. London, 1950.

North, C. C.: *Social Differentiation*. Chapel Hill, N. Carolina, 1926.

Park, R. E.: 'Personality and Cultural Conflict', *'Social Conflict': Papers presented to the Twenty-Fifth Annual Meeting of the American Sociological Society held at Cleveland, December 1930*. Chicago, 1931.

Plant, J. S.: *Personality and the Culture Pattern*. New York, 1937.

Rothacker, E.: *Schichten der Persönlichkeit*. Leipzig, 1937.

Schiffer, H.: *Die Politische Schulung des Englischen Volkes*. Leipzig, 1931.

Simmel, G.: *Soziologie*. Leipzig, 1908.
(Especially Chapters 6 and 9.)

Sullivan, H. S.: 'Psychiatry. Introduction to the Study of Interpersonal Relations', *Psychiatry*, Vol. 1.

Thomas, W. I., and Thomas, D. S.: *The Child in America: Behaviour Problems and Programs*. New York, 1932.

Volkart, E. H. (Ed.): *Social Behaviour and Personality: Contributions of W. I. Thomas to Theory and Social Research*. New York, 1951.

D. Individualisation and Socialisation

Burgess, E. W.: *The Function of Socialisation in Social Evolution*. Chicago, 1916.

Cooley, C. H.: *Human Nature and the Social Order*. New York, Chicago, 1928.
(Especially Chapters III, IV, V, VI and X.)

Dewey, J.: *Human Nature and Conduct*. New York, 1930.

Mead, G. H.: *Mind, Self and Society*. Chicago, 1933.

Ross, E. A.: *The Outlines of Sociology*. London, New York, 1933.

Smith, W. R.: *Principles of Educational Sociology*. Boston, New York, 1929.

Spykman, N. J.: *The Social Theory of Georg Simmel*. Chicago, 1925.
(Especially Book I, Chapters I and VII.)

CHAPTER VI: E. COMPETITION AND MONOPOLY

Cooley, C. H.: *Sociological Theory and Social Research*. New York, 1930.

Cooley, C. H.: *The Social Process*. New York, 1927.
(Especially Chapters IV, V, VIII, XII and XXXII.)

Horney, K.: *The Neurotic Personality of Our Time*. London, 1937.

May, M. A., and Doob, L.: 'Competition and Co-operation', *Social Science Research Council Bulletin*, No. 25, 1937.

Oppenheimer, F.: *System der Soziologie*. Jena, 1922–27.

Reaney, M. J.: 'The Psychology of the Organised Group Game', *British Journal of Psychology*, Monograph Supplements, Vol. 4, Cambridge.

Schiffer, H.: *Die Politische Schulung des Englischen Volkes*. Leipzig, 1931.

Sombart, W.: *Das Wirtschaftsleben im Zeitalter des Kapitalismus. Hochkapitalismus: II Halbband*. Leipzig, 1924.

Tawney, R. H.: *The Acquisitive Society*. London, 1921.

Veblen, T.: 'Christian Morality and the Competitive System', *International Journal of Ethics*, Vol. 20, 1920.

Watson, G.: 'The Measurement of Fair Mindedness', *Teachers' College Contributions to Education*, No. 176, New York, 1925.

Wiese, L. v., and Becker, H.: *Systematic Sociology*. New York, 1932.
(Especially Chapters VIII and X.)

Whittemore, I. C.: 'The Competitive Consciousness', *Journal of Abnormal and Social Psychology*, Vol. 20, April 1925.

Wright, H. W.: 'Rational Self-Interest and Social Adjustment', *International Journal of Ethics*, Vol. 30, 1919–20.

CHAPTER VII: COMPETITION AND CO-OPERATION

F. Selection

G. The Main Effects of Competition and Selection on Mental Life

Cooley, C. H.: *Social Process*. New York, 1927
(Especially Part I, Chapter IV and Part V, Chapter XII.)

Hartshorne, E. J.: *German Youth and the Nazi Dream of Victory*. New York and Toronto, 1941.

Ichheiser, G.: *Die Kritik des Erfolges*. Leipzig, 1930.

Mannheim, K.: 'Competition as a Cultural Phenomenon'.
(See *Essays on the Sociology of Knowledge*. London, 1952.)

158

Pillsbury, W. B.: 'Selection—an Unnoticed Function of Education', *Scientific Monthly*. January 1921.

Sorokin, P. A.: *Social Mobility*. New York and London, 1927.

Thurnwald, R.: 'Führerschaft und Siebung', *Zeitschrift für Völkerpsychologie und Soziologie*, Jg. 2, 1926.

H. Co-operation and the Division of Labour

Bouglé, C.: 'Théories sur la Division du Travail', *L'Année Sociologique*, Vol. VI, Paris, 1903.

Bücher, K.: *Die Entstehung der Volkswirtschaft*. Tübingen, 1920.

Durkheim, E.: *De la Division du Travail Social*. Paris, 1922. (Especially Book I, Chapters II and III.)

Hughes, E. C.: 'Personality Types and the Division of Labour'.
(See Burgess, E. W. (Ed.): *Personality and the Social Group*. Chicago, 1929.)

Kropotkin, P.: *Mutual Aid a Factor of Evolution*. New York, 1922.

May, M., and Doob, L. W.: 'Competition and Cooperation', *Social Science Research Bulletin*. New York, 1937.

Mayo, E.: *Human Problems of Industrial Civilization*. New York, 1933.

Mead, M. (Ed.): *Coöperation and Competition among Primitive Peoples*. London, 1937.

Tylor, E. B.: *Primitive Culture*. New York, 1924.

Ward, H. F.: *The New Social Order*. New York, 1919.

Ward, H. F.: *In Place of Profits*. New York, 1933.

PART 3

SOCIAL INTEGRATION

CHAPTER VIII: A. THE SOCIOLOGY OF GROUPS

1. The Crowd. 2. The Public. 3. Abstract Masses and the Abstract Public. 4. Organised Groups

Blumer, H.: 'Collective Behaviour'.
(See Park, R. E. (Ed.): *Outline of the Principles of Sociology*. New York, 1939.)

Clark, C. D.: 'The Concept of the Public', *Southwestern Social Science Quarterly.* 1933.

Dewey, J.: *The Public and its Problems.* New York, 1927.

La Pierre, R. T.: *Collective Behaviour.* New York, 1938.

Le Bon, G.: *The Crowd.* New York, 1925.

MacIver, R. M.: *Society: a Textbook of Sociology.* New York, 1937.
(Especially Chapters X, XI and XII.)

Martin, E. D.: *The Behaviour of Crowds.* New York, 1920.

Ross, E. A.: *Social Psychology.* New York, 1909.

Sherif, M.: *The Psychology of Social Norms.* New York, 1936.

Simmel, G.: 'Persistence of Social Groups' (translated by A. Small), *American Journal of Sociology*, Volumes 3 and 4, 1897-8, 1898-9.

Young, K.: *Sourcebook for Social Psychology.* New York, 1933.

CHAPTER IX. THE SOCIOLOGY OF GROUPS
(*Continued*)

5. The Types of Groupings

Beaver, A. P.: 'The Initiation of Social Contacts by Pre-school Children', *Child Development Monographs*, No. 7, New York, 1932.

Bernard, L. L.: 'Conflict Between Primary Group Attitudes and Derivative Group Ideals in Modern Society', *American Journal of Sociology*, Vol. 41, 1935–36.

Burgess, E.: 'The Family and the Person'.
(See Burgess, E. W. (Ed.): *Personality and the Social Group.* Chicago, 1929.)

Dewey, J.: *School and Society.* Chicago, 1910.

Ellwood, C. A.: *The Psychology of Human Society.* New York, 1925.

Folsom, J. K.: *The Family and Democratic Society.* New York, 1932.

Hocking, W. E.: *Morale—Its Meaning.* New Haven, 1918.

Simmel, G.: *Soziologie.* Leipzig, 1908.
(Especially Chapters 2, 8 and 10.)

Simmel, G.: 'The Number of Members as Determining the Sociological Form of the Group' (translated by A. Small), *American Journal of Sociology*, Vol. 8, 1902–03.

Simmel, G.: 'The Persistence of the Social Group' (translated by A. Small), *American Journal of Sociology*, Vol. 3, 1897–98 and Vol. 4, 1898–99.

Smith, W. R.: *An Introduction to Educational Sociology.* Boston and New York, 1929.

Spykman, N. J.: *The Social Theory of Georg Simmel.* Chicago, 1925.
(Especially Chapters I, III and VII in Book II.)

Sumner, G. W.: *Folkways.* Boston, 1907.

Thrasher, F. M.: *The Gang.* Chicago, 1925.

Tönnies, F.: *Community and Association* (translated by C. P. Loomis). London, 1955.

Wiese, L. v., and Becker, H.: *Systematic Sociology.* New York, 1932.
(Especially Chapters XXXIV–XLI.)

6. *The State*

Lowie, R. H.: *The Origin of the State.* New York, 1927.

MacIver, R. M.: *The Modern State.* Oxford, 1926.

Oppenheimer, F.: *The State* (translated by J. M. Gittermann). Indianapolis, 1914.

Sumner, W. G., and Keller, A. G.: *The Science of Society.* New Haven, 1927.
(Especially Vol. I, Part III, Chapter XVI.)

Weber, Max: *Essays in Sociology From Max Weber* (translated and ed. by H. H. Gerth and C. W. Mills). London, New York, 1947.

Weber, Max: *The Theory of Social and Economic Organisation.* Being Part I of *Wirtschaft und Gesellschaft* (translated by A. R. Henderson and T. Parsons). London, 1947.
(Especially Chapters I and III.)

CHAPTER X. B. THE CLASS PROBLEM

Beard, C. and M. R.: *The Rise of American Civilisation.* New York, 1936.

Briefs, G.: 'Das Gewerbliche Proletariat', *Grundriss der Sozialökonomik.* Part IX/1. Tübingen, 1925.

Carr-Saunders, A. M., and Caradoc Jones, D.: *A Survey of the Social Structure of England and Wales.* London, 1927.

Cooley, C. H.: *Social Organisation.* New York, 1922.

Dollard, J.: *Caste and Class in a Southern Town*. New Haven, 1937.

Ginsberg, M.: *Sociology*. London, 1934.

Hobhouse, L. T.: *Morals in Evolution*. London, 1915.

Hobhouse, L. T.: *The Making of Man*. New York, 1931.

Klineberg, O.: *Race Differences*. New York, 1935.

Laski, H.: *The Modern State in Theory and Practice*. London, 1935.

Marshall, T. H.: 'Social Class—A Preliminary Analysis', *Sociological Review*, Vol. 26, 1934.

Marshall, T. H. (Ed.): *Class Conflict and Social Stratification*. London, 1939.

Marx, K.: *Das Kapital*. Vol. III, Chicago, 1909.

Marx, K., and Engels, F.: *The Communist Manifesto*. London, 1883.

Mosca, G.: *The Ruling Class*. New York, 1939.

Mukerji, D. G.: *Caste and Outcaste*. New York, 1923.

Sorokin, P.: *Social Mobility*. London and New York, 1927.

Speier, H.: 'Social Stratification in the Urban Community', *American Sociological Review*, Vol. 1, 1936.

Veblen, T. B.: *The Theory of the Leisure Class*. New York, 1925.

Weber, Max: *The Theory of Social and Economic Organisation*. Being Part I of *Wirtschaft und Gesellschaft* (translated by A. R. Henderson and T. Parsons). London, 1947. (Especially Chapter IV.)

Warner, W. L.: 'American Caste and Class', *American Journal of Sociology*, Vol. 42, 1936–37.

PART 4

SOCIAL STABILITY AND SOCIAL CHANGE

CHAPTER XI: FACTORS OF SOCIAL STABILITY

1. Social Control and Authority

Benne, K. D.: 'A Conception of Authority. An Introductory Study', Teachers College, Columbia University, *Contributions to Education*. New York, 1943.

BIBLIOGRAPHY

Cooley, C. H.: *The Social Process*. New York, 1927.
(Especially Parts I and II.)

Davis, J., and Barnes, H. E., et al.: *An Introduction to Sociology*. New York, 1927.
(Especially Book II, Part IV.)

Ross, E. A.: *Social Control*. New York, 1901.
(Especially Chapters X–XIX.)

Stern, L.: 'The Sociology of Authority', *Publications of the American Sociological Society*, Vol. 18.

Wallas, G.: *Our Social Heritage*. London, 1921.

Wooddy, C. H., and Stouffer, S. A.: 'Local Opinion and Public Opinion', *American Journal of Sociology*, Vol. 36, 1930–31.

2. *Custom. 3. Law as a Form of Social Control*

Ginsberg, M.: *Sociology*. London, 1934.
(Especially Chapter V.)

Maine, H.: *Ancient Law*. London, 1907.

Sumner, W. G.: *Folkways*. Boston, 1907.

4. *Prestige and Leadership*

Bogardus, E. S.: *Leaders and Leadership*. New York, 1934.

Gerth, H.: 'The Nazi Party: Its Leadership and Composition', *American Journal of Sociology*, Vol. 45, 1940.

MacIver, R. M.: *The Modern State*. Oxford, 1926.

Nicolson, H.: *The Meaning of Prestige*. Cambridge, 1937.

Pigors, P.: *Leadership and Domination*. London, 1936.

Waller, W.: *The Sociology of Teaching*. New York, 1932.
(Especially Chapter 16.)

Whitehead, T. N.: *Leadership in a Free Society*. Cambridge, 1937.

Speier, H.: 'Honor and Social Structure', *Social Research*, Vol. 2, 1935.

5. *The Philosophical and Sociological Interpretation of Values*

Burrow, T.: 'Social Images vs. Reality', *Journal of Abnormal and Social Psychology*, Vol. 19.

Chadwick, H. M.: *The Heroic Age*. Cambridge, 1926.

Cooley, C. H.: *Social Process*. New York, 1927.
(Especially Part VI.)

BIBLIOGRAPHY

Mannheim, K.: 'Sociology of Human Valuations'.
(See Dugdale, J. E. (Ed.): *Further Papers on the Social Sciences*. London, 1937.)
Weber, Max: *Religionssoziologie*, Vol. I, Tübingen, 1925.
Weber, Max: *The Protestant Ethic and the Spirit of Capitalism* (translated by T. Parsons). London, 1930.

CHAPTER XII: CAUSES OF SOCIAL CHANGE

Berthe, E.: *Du 'Capital' aux 'Réflexions sur la Violence'*. Paris, 1932.
Buber, M. M.: *Karl Marx's Interpretation of History*. Cambridge, Mass., 1927.
Dewey, J.: 'Authority and Resistance to Social Change', *School and Society*, Vol. 44, 1936.
Hobhouse, L. T.: *Social Evolution and Political Theory*. New York, 1922.
MacIver, R. M.: *Society: a Textbook of Sociology*. New York, 1937.
(Especially Book III.)
Mannheim, K.: *Man and Society in an Age of Reconstruction*. London, 1941.
Marx, Karl: *Zur Kritik der Politischen Ökonomie*. Berlin, 1859. Translated by N. Y. Stone, New York, 1904.
Ogburn, W. F.: *Social Change*. New York, 1929.
Ogburn, W. F.: 'Stationary and Changing Societies', *American Journal of Sociology*, Vol. 42, 1936–37.
Thornton, J. E. (Ed.): *Science and Social Change*. Washington, 1930.

Index of Names

Index of Subjects

166

INDEX OF SUBJECTS

INDEX OF SUBJECTS

INDEX OF SUBJECTS

CPSIA information can be obtained
at www.ICGtesting.com
Printed in the USA
BVHW071453311218
536776BV00010B/647/P